SYONAN
MY STORY

SYONAN

MY STORY

THE JAPANESE OCCUPATION OF SINGAPORE

MAMORU SHINOZAKI

Marshall Cavendish
Editions

Design by Steven Tan
© Mamoru Shinozaki
First published in 1975 by Asia Pacific Press Pte Ltd. Published by Times Books
International in 1982. Reprinted 1984, 1992, 1995, 2001, 2006

This edition published in 2011 by
Marshall Cavendish Editions
An imprint of Marshall Cavendish International
1 New Industrial Road, Singapore 536196

Other Marshall Cavendish Offices:
Marshall Cavendish International. PO Box 65829, London EC1P 1NY, UK •
Marshall Cavendish Corporation. 99 White Plains Road, Tarrytown NY 10591-9001,
USA • Marshall Cavendish International (Thailand) Co Ltd. 253 Asoke, 12th Flr,
Sukhumvit 21 Road, Klongtoey Nua, Wattana, Bangkok 10110, Thailand •
Marshall Cavendish (Malaysia) Sdn Bhd, Times Subang, Lot 46, Subang Hi-Tech
Industrial Park, Batu Tiga, 40000 Shah Alam, Selangor Darul Ehsan, Malaysia

Marshall Cavendish is a trademark of Times Publishing Limited

National Library Board (Singapore) Cataloguing in Publication Data
Shinozaki, Mamoru, 1908-1991.
Syonan : my story : the Japanese occupation of Singapore / Mamoru Shinozaki. –
Singapore : Marshall Cavendish Editions, 2011.
p. cm.
ISBN : 978-981-4328-52-4
1. Shinozaki, Mamoru, 1908-1991. 2. World War, 1939-1945 – Personal narratives,
Japanese. 3. World War, 1939-1945 – Campaigns – Malay Peninsula. 4. Singapore
– History – Siege, 1942.
5. Singapore – History – Japanese occupation, 1942-1945. I. Title.

D811.5
940.548252 — dc22   OCN665581494

Printed in Singapore by KWF Printing Pte Ltd

to the war victims

CONTENTS

	Foreword by H.E. Wilson	8
	Introduction by Yap Pheng Geck	11
1	Changi Prison	16
2	Outbreak of War	27
3	Chinese Massacre	40
4	Overseas Chinese Association	50
5	Assignment in Syonan	57
6	Lady Thomas	65
7	General Yamashita	68
8	$50 Million Donation	74
9	Japanese Influx	82
10	Military Administration	90
11	Indian Independence League	96
12	Death Railway	103
13	Allied War Heroes	108
14	Evacuation of Syonan: Endau	116
15	Evacuation of Syonan: Bahau	131
16	Another Surrender	137
17	Japanese Repatriation	144
18	Dr Paglar's Treason Trial	150
19	War Crimes Trials	154
20	Episodes	169

FOREWORD

The occupation of Singapore was, for those who survived it, a profoundly traumatic experience. Many, of course, did not survive it at all; and memories of mass murders and senseless brutalities perpetuate bitterness and antagonism which, although understandable, nevertheless tend to conceal aspects of the period which deserve to be seen in clearer perspective. It is as well to recall that not all atrocities were committed on one side or by a single race, and that such incidents are symptomatic of the moral degeneracy of man at war.

Few official records and reports survived the war, and for this reason if no other it is fortunate that Mr Shinozaki has decided to publish his recollections of those fateful days. Before the war, he was a Press Attaché at the Japanese Consulate in Singapore. After his release from Changi Prison (where he was serving a sentence for espionage), he became a senior official of the Syonan Tokubetsu Shi (Singapore City Government), serving initially as Director of Education and later as Head of the Welfare Department. In the former post he was instrumental in restoring a degree of order to the war-torn island school system, and in the latter, it fell to his lot to organize the settlements at Endau and Bahau. Mr Shinozaki's account of these and many other aspects of the administration of occupied Singapore provide a new and often provocative view of a period about which all too little is known.

It was, of course, impossible for any civil servant to reverse the madness of instructions emanating from a military authority which had long nurtured a sense of grievance against the Chinese of Singapore but part of the fascination of the author's version of the events stems from the way it reveals the reactions of an intelligent and sensitive young man to a horrifying situation, and how he was impelled—at considerable personal risk—to do what he could to ameliorate the physical suffering and mental anguish of so many. When, for example, the history of that much-aligned organization, the Overseas Chinese Association, comes to be written, there is little doubt that Mr Shinozaki will be seen to have played a vital told in its formation and function as a shield (or 'cape') behind which so many sought protection. Again, Mr Shinozaki's decision to supply rice to communist guerrillas of the Malayan People's Anti-Japanese Army in return for the protection of Chinese settlers at Endau could hardly have been calculated to endear him to his more zealous compatriots, had it become known.

Mr Shinozaki writes with perception and humour without attempting to conceal the harsh realities of the situation. His story is necessarily anecdotal at times, and always distinctively personal; but its publication will provide a valuable source of material for all who are interested in a period which not only marked the effective end of colonialism in Singapore, but which also prompted in prototype so many of the features of a new and vitally dynamic city-state which was to become present-day Singapore.

H.E. Wilson
University of British Columbia,
Vancouver, Canada
1975

INTRODUCTION

I deem it a privilege extended to me to contribute this brief introduction to the story of Syonan as told by Mr M. Shinozaki. Reading through the pages I felt as if I was reliving the days of the Japanese occupation all over again, but without the fears and anxieties that harassed me then.

Throughout the Japanese occupation I was in Singapore under strict surveillance by the Japanese Military Police (the Kempei Tai) because I was a senior officer of the Straits Settlements Volunteer Force, which the Japanese invaders mistook for the DALFORCE, their enemy No. 1 among the Singapore residents. In Japanese the term 'volunteer' is synonymous with 'guerrilla', the most hated and dreaded by the Japanese soldiers because of their bitter experience in China. I had then the misfortune of being popularly known as the Captain of the Chinese Volunteers and this caused the Japanese Military Police to pay particular attention to all my movements.

Although I had no contact with Mr Shinozaki until the latter part of the occupation and only during the Endau days, I was nevertheless a witness to or had personal knowledge of the many of the scenes and events recounted by him in his book and I know personally many of the people who had been helped by him in one way or another. In fact I personally know every local leader named in his narrative, many of who are now long dead and gone. I can therefore in all sincerity vouch for his genuineness and his untiring helpfulness particularly towards the Chinese community whom he knew had been singled out for special persecution.

I have seen Mr Shinozaki at work at Toyo Hotel in Queen Street where he moved freely and busily among swarms of desperate-looking people pestering him for all manner of help. I have watched him closely in Endau moving unostentatiously among labourers and settlers like any one of the evacuees. He was so different from the other Japanese, military or civilian, during the occupation. I truly believe that he had totally identified himself with the people of Singapore under the compulsion of his inborn compassion for suffering humanity.

I also know that he was not popular with the military authorities. He was under suspicion by the Kempei Tai and was hated and ostracized in certain Japanese circles. In fact my Japanese mentors had cautioned me to keep aloof from Mr Shinozaki so as to avoid further complications with the Japanese military.

I have seen literature about the atrocities of the Kempei Tai and the Occupation Forces. I have yet to come across any book which objectively portrays the life of the people of Singapore during the Japanese occupation—a people who despite untold hardships and suffering kept up their spirit and their faith that the reign of terror could not last, that the tide of battles must turn and that they would live to see deliverance. Mr Shinozaki must have been sympathetically aware that there was no welcome for Japanese rule in Singapore. His story of Syonan, I think, comes very close to such a book.

I particularly value the references to Dr Lim Boon Keng and Dr C.J. Paglar. His narration of their plight moved me deeply for I was in the know about the cases of the two ill-fated leaders. In telling about these two leaders, Mr Shinozaki was in fact explaining the role of our community leaders under the trying conditions of the occupation—to yield in order to conquer, to submit so as to save the lives of one's fellowmen. Our community leaders were never quislings to the Japanese conquerors. Many of them were veritable Daniels in the lion's den.

Mr Shinozaki has freely mentioned names, dates and places in his book. The veracity of all this can readily be checked. The whole story is to me a truthful and unvarnished account of the conditions and the life in Singapore during the Japanese occupation.

The people of war-time Singapore owe much to Mr Shinozaki. This is my testimony.

Yap Pheng Geck
1975

ACKNOWLEDGEMENTS

I would like to thank Mr H.E. Wilson who wrote the foreword for this book and Dr Yap Pheng Geck for his introduction. I would also like to thank Mr Hugh Savage and Mr Alex Josey for reading the manuscripts and for their invaluable comments. I am indebted to many others, too numerous to name, but a special word of thanks to Miss Dora Ho for typing the first draft of my story.

Mamoru Shinozaki

1
CHANGI PRISON

On 10 September 1940, almost exactly a year and three months before Japan invaded the Malay Peninsula, Colonel T. Tanikawa, the planning chief of Japan's Imperial Army headquarters in Tokyo, arrived in Singapore.

He was accompanied by Major Kunitake. Later, Major Kunitake became a staff officer of the 25th Army under General Yamashita. This was the Japanese army that attacked Malaya and Singapore.

Colonel Tanikawa and Major Kunitake wanted to travel along the Malayan coasts, both east and west. Their purpose was to investigate the condition of the coasts. I had been requested to take them there.

First we toured Singapore. We travelled along the coast road, going through Katong, Siglap and Changi to Pasir Panjang. We skirted Tengah Air Base, then still under construction. Later we drove along Bukit Timah Road to Johore Bahru, and then to Kota Tinggi, Mersing and Endau.

The next day we went to Malacca.

On the night of 13 September we returned to Singapore and went to the home of Mr Yamakawa. Mr Yamakawa had been a Japanese Army captain during the Russo-Japanese war. Captured by a Russian warship after his transport ship sank in action, he was taken to Petrograd (now Leningrad). When the war ended he was sent home but on the way he landed in Singapore. He fell in love with the place and decided to make Singapore his home. He had lived there ever since.

At Yamakawa's house a map was spread out before us. Colonel Tanikawa declared, 'It's impossible to attack Singapore from the sea, that is, from the east, south or west. Attack is possible only from the Johore Strait north of Singapore.'

The next day the two Japanese officers returned to Tokyo. That evening I received a telephone message from Mr A.E.G. Blades, the Japanese-speaking head of the Special Branch, Singapore Police. I was requested to report to his office at nine o' clock the next morning. I was not altogether surprised. I had been shadowed by detectives for some time.

I tried to get in touch with Mr Toyoda, the consul-general, but he was not in, Fearing the worst, I went to my old friend Mr Yamakawa to bid him goodbye.

It was not until after the war that I learnt that the two officers I had taken round Malaya and Singapore in September 1940 had passed on their advice to Lieutenant-Colonel Tsuji, chief planner in General Yamashita's army. Tsuji admitted as much in his book when he wrote 'The south and east seafronts of Singapore are strongly defended. There are no fortifications in strength on the

Johore side. The R.A.F. is not as strong as the newspapers say. The number of troops in Kedah is increasing.'

I was taken into Mr Blades' room by Inspector Donough. Mr Blades took me to the office of the Acting Colonial Secretary, Mr Weizberg, in Empress Place. Weizberg gave me no more than a glance and left the room. I looked at the paintings of the British Governors on the walls, and reflected on past British colonial policy.

Suddenly I heard angry voices in the adjacent room. I recognized the voice of Mr Toyoda. The other voice I assumed to be that of Mr Weizberg. He was saying, 'On the instructions of my Government I will detain Shinozaki. I intend to have his room at the Japanese Consulate searched.'

'This is against international law,' retorted the consul-general. 'You can't do this.'

'You have no extra-territorial rights in the Consulate,' declared Mr Weizberg. 'I will carry out my orders from London.'

'It's war then,' the consul-general shouted, and left the room.

I did not see Mr Weizberg again until some months later, shortly after the Japanese had captured Singapore. He was walking bare-footed, looking tired and old, along Bras Basah Road. I returned to my hotel, bought a pair of shoes and a bottle of whisky, took them to Bishop Devals and asked him to give them to Mr Weizberg.

The police searched my room after my arrest but failed to find any incriminating documents. Then Mr Blades picked up the memo-calendar on my desk. This was where I wrote down my appointments. As he picked it up

I could not help whispering to myself, 'My God!' Blades saw my lips move and said, 'Very good.' I was taken to the Central Police Station where I was detained for several days in a dark, iron-barred cell.

I slept most of the first day. The following day Inspector Donough took me to Mr Blades for interrogation. This lasted a few days. Then I was taken to Outram Prison, an old and gloomy building built in 1840. It has since been pulled down and replaced by high-rise flats. When the large iron gates swung open some prisoners clustered round, greeting me with 'Hi! Japan!'

I was put in a room in a block away from the others. It was clean and comfortable; there was a shower. I stayed for a month, pending trial. I was allowed books, and food was sent in from outside. But I had no news from the outside world.

I attended a preliminary inquiry at the District Court, and later I appeared in the Supreme Court charged with collecting information which might be useful to a foreign power. The trial lasted a week. I was found guilty on two charges. On one I was sentenced to three years' hard labour and on the other, to six months' imprisonment.

I was not, of course, a spy. I was a press attaché. My duties called for me to maintain good relations with the press and also to keep a press clippings file. This was what the Special Branch called 'information which might be useful to a foreign country'. On instructions from Tokyo the press clippings file contained a great deal of information on a wide variety of subjects. But all this information had, of course, appeared in the local press at some time or other.

At the trial the prosecution made much of the fact that I often met British soldiers. I did, but there was nothing sinister about that. I met many people.

Relations between Japan and Britain were worsening at the time. A few weeks before my arrest, Mr Cooks of Reuters had been arrested in Tokyo by the *Kempei Tai* (the Military Police). He committed suicide by jumping out of a window of the Kempei Tai headquarters. In retaliation Mr Kobayashi of *Domei* had been arrested in Singapore. Shortly afterwards I was arrested. I was thirty-two at the time of my arrest.

After my trial I was put into a black maria with other convicted men and returned to Outram Prison. This, I thought to myself, is where I must live for the next three and a half years. I was ordered to change into prison garb. It had a number on it—L404.

They gave me a piece of bread. Then I was taken to a dark and tiny cell, about three metres by two metres. In the middle was a concrete bed. In the corner were two buckets of water. One was to drink from; the other was for toilet purposes. This was a cell without electric light. At night, when there was a moon, moonbeams would float through a small window. That night I slept badly.

At half-past five the next morning a warden unlocked the cell door. 'Come out with your toilet bucket,' he ordered. Prisoners trooped out from their cells, each with his bucket. There we stood for roll-call and inspection. Then we marched away to empty the buckets. Immediately upon our return we were given a bowl of rice gruel without salt. I could not touch mine.

The following day the long-term prisoners—I was among them—were removed to Changi Prison. We travelled in black marias. Through the windows I could see people moving on the streets. To one locked up, they all looked happy. At least they were free. I felt dejected, humiliated. My name had become a number. I wished then that I had been shot, not sentenced to imprisonment.

Changi Prison is a jail with tall double walls. In the front is a clock tower. As we entered I saw that it was exactly 11 a.m.

Soon after the Japanese invasion of Singapore, British civilian prisoners and British troops were imprisoned there. After the Japanese surrender, Japanese war criminals occupied the cells. More than 130 Japanese were hanged after climbing the thirteen fateful steps to the gallows at the east corner of Changi Prison.

After the clerk had read out the prison regulations I was taken to the E block. That was the block for European prisoners. Here the cells were wider and cleaner than at Outram. There was a toilet and a bookcase in the corner, and a bed with a mattress. We were given a toothbrush every third month, half a cake of soap every fortnight, and a change of clothes twice a week. After the daily morning inspection we were allowed to walk in the prison yard for half an hour.

Early on my first morning in Changi, as I looked up at the crimson sky, way out in the South China Sea, I though of Japan, my country, far to the north-east, and I composed this Chinese poem:

> *Alone in Singapore*
> *No merit, yet in jail*
> *Look for north-east in dawn light*
> *Bow my head in heartbreak!*

Breakfast was at 7 a.m.—a cup of weak tea, three small pieces of bread and a little jam. Immediately after breakfast we went to the workshop where we worked until noon. I was the only Asian prisoner among Europeans and Eurasians. One of my fellow convicts was Captain-Engineer Loveday. He was serving four and a half years for corruption.

Then there was MacDonald, chief engineer of a mine, Kershaw, Bennett and others. They were all in jail for corruption. There were some soldiers serving sentences for desertion, and there was a Highlander whom I remember as John. He was in for life for murdering his friend in Shanghai. John was a rough and desperate character, and his Scottish accent made it difficult for me to understand him. Nevertheless, we often held long conversations. He would talk of his old mother and his young sister in Scotland. He knew he would never see them again. Even when he laughed I could detect a note of desperation.

I tried to put aside my own thoughts by concentrating on my prison task; on a sewing machine I repaired mailbags. Smoking and reading helped to break the monotony of prison routine. After a day's work, at 5 p.m., we would gather at the E block to get our ration of three small pieces of bread. At the same time we were given three cigarettes and three matches. This was a happy moment for me because I could anticipate the pleasure of smoking the cigarettes in my cell. Every evening I would split each match with a pin, thus making three matches out of one. This operation required considerable patience because it involved splitting the head of the match. Once I had done this I was assured of nine separate smokes until lights out at nine o' clock.

Never at any time did I smoke more than a third of a cigarette. I smoked and read from five o' clock until nine o' clock every day. These were hours of comparative pleasure— the most satisfying part of my life in jail. I swore I would never give up smoking, ever!

But six months later the cigarette ration was suddenly stopped when I was transferred from the E block to the Asian block. In a prison in Japan a British officer had been badly treated. The British retaliated by punishing me. Not only was my cigarette ration stopped, my diet was also changed. I was given a bowl of rice gruel without salt in the morning, a bowl of unpolished rice with a small quantity of salt-fish for lunch, and another bowl of unpolished rice with salt-fish for my evening meal.

I missed the cigarettes most of all. After five o' clock when the fragrance of cigarettes being enjoyed by others came into my cell it was all I could do not to stand up and scream for just one puff.

Occasionally a warden threw me a cigarette. I wonder if he could have known how grateful I was. It was a young Chinese in the next cell who made life tolerable after a while. His name was Chen. He passed me a cigarette and a match one morning after inspection. I thanked him and asked how he had managed to keep it hidden during inspection. He said, 'I grip it in my crotch.' I hid it in the lining of my shirt while we were being marched off to the workshop. Once again I had my five o' clock smoke. It meant a lot to me.

Chen continued to give me cigarettes. Sometimes they were damp with his perspiration. I did not care. I shall never forget Chen's kindness.

Not only was my cigarette ration stopped and my food changed. Another harsh reprisal was the restriction of my reading. I had arranged for hundred of books to be sent to me in the Asian block. I was allowed no more than three I chose *Old Chinese Poetry* by Dr Kano, *International Public Law in War-time* by Dr Tateno and *Nanking Road* by Vicki Baum.

I was particularly attracted to *Nanking Road*. It was written just after the Chinese revolution. It was the story of a young Chinese who married a French girl during his stay in Paris. He returned to China after the civil war began. I still remember a remark made by one of the characters in the book: 'A dog during peace is better off than a man during war.' These three books became my best friends.

Life in Changi Prison was monotonously simple. Every day was like the other. There were no celebrations, not even on New Year's Day. The food was the same every morning—saltless rice gruel. When salt-fish was served I would try to keep the head to suck the following morning. Midday meals and evening meals were usually the same: *ikan bilis* (tiny salted fish), or bean spouts. I believe the prison authorities were allowed eight cents per prisoner for food at that time. We were always hungry. When hunger woke us up at night we filled out empty stomachs with water.

New prisoners came in during the evenings. Those prisoners who had completed their sentences were released in the mornings. It touched me deeply to see them go. I composed the following poem in Chinese:

Yesterday new convicts came in at evening bell
Morning saw old prisoners leave
So lonely I dwell
No Spring during three years in jail
Cherry blossoms in Japan: when will I hail?

I composed many Chinese poems. I scratched them on the ground during my walks in the prison yard or on walls. There was nowhere else to write them. We had no writing materials in jail.

Prisoners were not allowed to receive visitors during the first six months of their sentences. When that time was up, the Japanese consul-general, Mr Tsurumi, came to see me. He stayed for half an hour. He told me that Japan, Germany and Italy had formed an alliance. Relations between Britain and Japan had deteriorated.

I did not realize it at that time, but my stay in Changi Prison was actually providing me with very valuable experience, for after the Japanese invasion, I became an administrator in the City Government of Singapore (*Syonan Tokubetsu Shi*). In prison I learnt a great deal about human relations. Nobody puts on airs or graces in prison. Everyone is forced to behave naturally. In Changi there were many races with many different customs and relations, but there were no social distinctions, no classes. We were all prisoners serving in the same conditions.

For example, we showered together every day; 400 of us gathered under a long water-pipe punched full of holes. We would march there from work. Sitting or standing beneath the pipe with a piece of soap in our hands, we waited for the water to be turned on. The water flowed for a short while, about five or six minutes, then it would be turned off. Once it started, everyone would be madly busy, scrubbing their emaciated bodies with pieces of rags cut from gunny sacks.

There were many other prison experiences which taught me much about human relationship. They all stood me in good stead when I became a city adminstrator.

2
OUTBREAK OF WAR

At about 4.30 in the morning of 8 December 1941, all the anti-aircraft guns around Changi Prison opened fire. They were marking the outbreak of World War Two in the Pacific.

I was taken to Captain Lily, the superintendent of the prison, and told that as Japan had declared war on Britain I would be treated as a prisoner of war. He said I would be put in a special detention cell.

My new cell was small and iron-barred and it reminded me of a bird cage. For some strange reason it was called Canji House. No longer did I go to the workshop. I was kept in my cell all day except for two half-hour spells for exercise. I walked about briskly. The rest of the day I sat in my cell awaiting my destiny.

Fortunately, I could see the sky from my cell. I spent some time observing the activities in the sky. I could see the Japanese bombers flying over Changi. As the anti-aircraft guns fired, a screen of grey dots could be seen against the blue of the sky. Some Japanese aircraft dived and released bombs, others made low-level runs. I heard bombs explode, and could see flames and smoke shoot up where they had dropped. I felt and heard the rumble of the ground when some of the bombs dropped near the prison. Not far away were military barracks.

Within a short while, all Japanese civilians in Singapore were interned at Changi Prison, including Mr Okamoto, the last consul-general. He and his staff were all lodged in the European E block. The other Japanese civilians were put in the Asian block. We convicted prisoners were returned to Outram Prison.

A few days before we went back to Outram, I heard the sharp whistle of a destroyer. This was about midnight on 11 December. I thought then that this was the British Z fleet (H.M.S. *Prince of Wales*, H.M.S. *Repulse* and four escort destroyers) leaving Singapore for the north-east coast of Malaya to attack the Japanese invasion fleet. Later I was to learn that this was not so. In fact, the two British warships had already been sunk by Japanese bombers off Kuantan. The sharp whistle was the sad signal of one of the returning destroyers. The destruction of the Z fleet stunned the British community. Prison warders appeared crestfallen and dejected.

On 19 December, the Japanese 25th Army occupied Penang. Prison warders in Penang were evacuated to Singapore. All the warders, perhaps naturally, became irritable and prone to anger.

Once again we convicted prisoners were sent back to Changi after the Japanese civilian detainees were transferred to India. This time, we saw from our black marias that most of the shop fronts had been boarded up. There were few people in the streets other than firemen hurrying from one fire to another. Overhead a British Brewster Buffalo and a Japanese fighter fought an air battle. It was an unequal fight; soon the Brewster was plunging to the ground, a heavy pall of smoke trailing behind.

On 11 January Japanese troops entered Kuala Lumpur. Twenty days later they were in Johore Bahru. During this period, Captain Lily, the prison superintendent, made a point of seeing me every morning. He would ask, 'How are you? Are you alright?' He was kind and sympathetic. One day he asked me if there was anything I wanted. I asked him for books and cigarettes. Later a warder brought both a tin of cigarettes and some books.

I made an effort to repay this kindness after Japanese troops invaded Singapore. I gave sweets to the children interned in Changi. Before the Japanese military authority took over the administration of the prison—while Japanese civil officers were in control—I had an opportunity of visiting Changi Prison and meeting Captain Lily, then a prisoner himself. We shook hands and I thanked him for his kindness when I was a prisoner. I gave him some tins of cigarettes. Shortly afterwards the Japanese military authority took over control of the prison. I was not allowed to visit Changi Prison again. I often wondered what became of Captain Lily.

On 7 February 1942, when I was still in Changi, a young warden named Shaw came to my cell with a tin of cigarettes. He said, 'My present to you. Take it. The fates are approaching. Goodbye.'

What did he mean? My fate? Was I to be shot? Or did he mean the collapse of Singapore? I did not know. Many of us thought that the collapse of Singapore was inevitable. What would happen to a Japanese convicted of espionage?

The night of 7 February was moonlit. No gunfire—an intense stillness. I could hear singing from the officers' mess. A farewell party? It seemed to me that the unbelievable was happening—the great British citadel of the East was on the eve of collapse. I composed a Chinese poem:

> Singapore surrounded by Japanese Imperial Army
> Moonlight shines over the island tonight
> British singing sad Lang Syne about their homes
> When the long expedition ends, so too must my life.

Could it be that the moon winked? I felt sad. The stillness accentuated my depression. Suddenly the British opened up a barrage at Johore Bahru on the Japanese preparing to cross the Straits to attack Singapore. The Japanese fired back. The noisy gun battle continued through the remainder of the night.

When the Japanese aircraft flew over, all the guns in Singapore stopped firing. They started again the moment the planes flew off. We all knew that the Japanese attack on Singapore had begun. I sat on the floor awaiting my fate. Would the British take me out and shoot me as a spy? If they did, how would I behave? Would I stand before the execution squad bravely awaiting the deadly volley? Would I be able to tear the bandage from my eyes and shout, 'Long live the Emperor'? These were my thoughts. I tried to remain calm.

Outside, for days the battle raged. At about five o' clock in the evening of 12 February it seemed that the fighting had even entered the prison. A Malay convict, Ah Long, rushed into my cell shouting, 'The Japanese are here! Come quickly!' I ran outside to find not Japanese troops but a group of convicts with rifles and pistols they had taken from the prison armoury.

At once I realized the danger. I shouted, 'Come here, everybody. You know I am a Japanese officer. You must obey my orders. Do you understand?'

They yelled back, 'Yes!'

I ordered them to put the rifles and the pistols in a heap at my feet. They did so.

There were about 700 prisoners in Changi Prison at that time, including some 30 Japanese, detained after the civilians had been sent to India. There were also a few old women, some Okinawan fishermen, Dr Nakamura from Malacca, and Masaji Hirayama. I told young Hirayama to collect the weapons and return them to the armoury.

Suddenly flames burst out form the top of the clock tower. I called for volunteers. Forty men answered my call and we soon had the fire under control and put it out.

From this tower, especially at night, we could get an excellent view of the battle for Singapore. Japanese gunfire seemed to be green, the answering fire from the British, yellow.

The firing line that day was in Bukit Timah. Changi was quiet. From the tower I was surprised to see a large group of Australian soldiers sitting in front of the prison gate. 'My God,' I thought, 'what next?' I could see that the

Highlanders' barracks at Selarang were on fire. Flames rose high into the sky.

Dr Nakamura and the old Japanese women had fashioned a Japanese flag out of a bedsheet. A rising sun had been etched on it in red ink. They had hung it on the main gate of the prison. I came down from the tower in a hurry and shouted, 'Australian soldiers outside! Pull down the flag!'

Women began to weep. Everybody became excited. I made sure that the gate was firmly secured. Some of the soldiers tried to force it open, but eventually they moved off.

I decided to check our water and food stocks. I stood in the centre of the courtyard and called on all prisoners to assemble before me, all 700 of them. There was, I discovered, enough food, but water was short. The Japanese had cut the water supply from Johore.

I guessed that the battle might go on for another month. Some of the prisoners were desperate criminals. How to maintain order among them until the proper authorities arrived to take over the prison?

I came down from the tower one day to find some of the prisoners looting the stores. Quick action was vital. I yelled, 'Hi! Anybody want to get out? I'll let you out of jail!' They came round me in a rush. Some of them had already packed looted goods on their shoulders. I told them they could go, but I warned them to be careful. Outside were many Australian soldiers. I told them that once outside the prison they could not return. Hirayama translated all I said into Malay.

There was a stampede for the main gate. Many of the prisoners were serving long sentences for murder, robbery, and other major crimes. About 500 of these prisoners streamed through the gates. I organized the 200 that remained into teams—a cooking team, a medical team, and a guards team. The aged and the women were put in the prison hospital.

Outside, the battle for Singapore continued, moving further and further from Changi, getting nearer and nearer to the city and the harbour.

At 7.30 in the evening of 15 February the noise of battle suddenly stopped. The blackness of the night and the stillness seemed to accentuate the enormous red flames shooting into the sky from the oil tanks. The moon was cloaked by thick smoke. In the clock tower of Changi Prison I took my first deep undisturbed sleep in four days.

About eight o' clock the next morning a car flying the rising sun flag stopped in front of the prison gate. I recognized the flag as the emblem of the Asahi newspaper. A Japanese stepped out of the car and called, 'Any Japanese inside? The British have surrendered.'

I shouted back that there were, and that I would open the gate. I talked to the Asahi war correspondent and he motored back to the city to report to the Kempei Tai. Within an hour the Kempai Tai were in Changi Prison, and we were taken to Beach Road, to the 2nd Field Military Kempei Tai headquarters. My rescue story was published in the Asahi and the Japanese Army newspapers. That was how many Japanese soldiers came to know my name.

Now the battle of the soldiers was over. The people's pain and suffering were about to begin—pillage, violence, slaughter.

Above: Changi Prison, where the author served his sentence for espionage.

Below: At the Japanese Consulate in Singapore in 1939, Mr and Mrs K. Toyoda (seated). Mr Nagao and the author (standing).

Attack was only possible from the north of Singapore. Japanese units
successfully advanced southward on bicycles. (Australian War Memorial)

Naval Base seen from Johore Bahru on 6 February 1942.
The Causeway had been cut off.

Above: General Yamashita at Bukit Timah Hill on 11 February 1942.

Below: The British marching to surrender on 15 Febrauary 1942.

Above: General Percival signing the surrender papers at Ford factory on 15 February 1942. From left to right: General Yamashita, Colonel Sugita (pointing) and Major-General Manaki. (Australia War Memorial)

Below: Selarang Barracks where some prisoners of war were interned during the occupation. (Australian War Memorial)

Scene of destruction from the top of Cathay Building facing Bras Basah Road,
16 February 1942.

3
CHINESE MASSACRE

Singapore was still burning when, with thirty other Japanese prisoners of Changi, I was driven in a military lorry to Beach Road. We saw nobody on the streets. Where was everybody?

At the Yokota Kempei Tai headquarters I was greeted by the unit's commander, Lieutenant-Colonel Yokota. He said that General Yamashita, concerned about the welfare of every Japanese, wanted to see me, but that first we would visit Colonel Oishi, the chief of the Kempei Tai. This was the man who was tried after the Japanese surrender as a war criminal, and hanged at Changi.

I went to Raffles College (now National University of Singapore) and paid my respects to General Yamashita and to Major-General Manaki, deputy chief of general staff of the 25th Imperial Army. Manaki had been the military attaché in Berlin before the war. I had also served in the Japanese Embassy in Berlin. We chatted for a while. He said he thought there were still some Germans in Singapore. He asked me to find them and protect them. He added that he was planning to set up a military administration and as I knew Singapore well, he sought my co-operation. I agreed to help him.

Then he went to Fort Canning which had been taken over as Defence headquarters by Major-General Kawamura. He was another general hanged at Changi after the war. The Kempei Tei was directly responsible to Defence headquarters, so Yokota reported to the major-general details of my activities at Changi.

Kawamura said, 'In battles soldiers have to make quick decisions. They can be arrogant and proud. Some find it difficult to adjust after the battle. You had better become an adviser at Defence headquarters, Foreign Affairs Department. This may make your task easier. You will also be able to help some of the army officers. Not all of them understand military law as applied to civilians. I request your help and protect good citizens.'

The major-general spoke softly. I saluted and said, 'Very well, Excellency.'

That night, 16 February 1942, I slept on the floor in what had been the Singapore Volunteers' headquarters in Beach Road. I shared the floor with scores of young Japanese officers and soldiers. All through the night they told me of their exploits during the fighting down the Malay Peninsula.

The following day, Lieutenant-Colonel Yokota and his staff moved to Toyo Hotel in Queen Street. Before the war this hotel had been owned by a Japanese. Yokota invited me to stay at the hotel with him. Japanese reporters came to the hotel to interview me.

I was still a Foreign Office official, so I sent a cable through *Domei* Newsagency to the Foreign Minister reporting conditions in Singapore. Back came instructions from the Ministry to contact the Swiss consul-general, take from him all relevant Japanese documents, and the Imperial Crest, and look after foreign interests. I contacted Mr Arbenz, the Swiss consul-general, and claimed the documents, and the key of the store where the belongings of the Japanese consul-general were kept. I gave Mr Arbenz a 'protection notice' for his residence and a special protective identification for him and his wife.

These notices and cards were necessary. Looters had already been busy. They had stripped many of the houses hurriedly vacated of furniture and anything else they could lay their hands on. They were Singaporeans, not soldiers. To me they all looked alike: bloodshot eyes, they wore singlets and shorts and rubber shoes. Some came in vans, station-wagons, or on foot carrying long poles to carry away their loot. Areas teeming with looters were the mainly European residential areas of Holland Road, Tanglin Road and Bukit Timah Road.

It seemed that nothing could stop them until one day eight looters broke into a Japanese military store. They were caught red-handed by soldiers. They were at once beheaded and their heads were put on spikes at eight different road junctions—at Tanjong Pagar, at Stamford Road, in Fullerton Square and elsewhere. This terrible lesson was effective. Looting stopped.

During much of this early period, ordinary Japanese soldiers were forbidden to enter the city which was guarded by the Kempei Tai and auxiliary military policemen from the Fifth Division. Singapore citizens could also not move around, especially at night.

I handed out protection passes to Germans, Italians, Swiss, Hungarians and Irish. Many Chinese asked the cook at Toyo Hotel, Tay Hon Jin, to persuade me to give them passes. I did. Chinese friends came to me direct for passes. I gave passes to members of religious organizations. Later literally thousands of people asked for these cards. I gave them out liberally. They were written in my own handwriting and stamped with my name and title—Special Foreign Affairs Officer, Defence Headquarters.

I did not bother to find out if those asking for passes were good citizens or bad hats. My only concern was to help as many people as I could in this confusion. The passes read: 'The bearer of this pass is a good citizen. Please look after him and protect him, and let him go about his business without hindrance.'

I was also able to help in other ways. An ammunition dump exploded at Geylang English School. Mr Chua Hoe Ann happened to be near by at the time. He was arrested by a guard and taken to Yokota Kempei Tai headquarters in Toyo Hotel. Fortunately for Mr Chua I was in the hotel at the time. I was able to secure his release.

On another occasion, Mr Mistri, proprietor of the Phoenix Aerated Water Factory was arrested by the Marine Kempei Tai and detained at the Tanjong Pagar

Police Station. His manager came to see me at Toyo Hotel, and I managed to get Mr Mistri freed.

Later, Mr Lim Soo Siam was arrested by the Y.M.C.A. Kempei Tai at Stamford Road. I got him released. Mr S.Q. Wong was detained at Fort Canning. I got him out. Mr Ong Ching Hway, Mr Pang Cheng Eng and many others were locked up in the Y.M.C.A. by the Kempei Tai. I managed to rescue them all. Because they had taken me from Changi Prison, the Kempei Tai knew me, and they respected me.

But when these members of the Kempei Tai were transferred, others took their places, and they knew nothing about me. Then things became much more difficult. I had much less influence with them.

For some time after the British surrender, shops were closed: shopkeepers were afraid of looters. There were dead bodies in the streets and in damaged buildings. The city was dirty and smelly: gas, water and electricity were in short supply, yet the fact that there was some gas, water and electricity was proof that a number of British engineers had remained at their posts in an effort to maintain these essential services.

When the time came to clear up the debris, clean the city and bury the dead, British health officers co-operated with Dr Ando, a well-known figure in pre-war Singapore. This team of British doctors worked hard for six months. During this time they stayed in the basement of what was then the Municipal Building, now the City Hall.

For a few days after the British surrender the emphasis was on cleaning up. Then, suddenly, the 25th Army head-quarters issued an astounding decree: all male Chinese in

Syonanto (Singapore) between the ages of 18 and 50 years were ordered to concentrate at five assembly points at noon on 21 February 1942. They were warned of severe punishment for disobedience. The five points were: the open area near Jalan Besar Stadium and the north end of Arab Street; the eastern end of River Valley Road near the junction of Clemenceau Avenue; the open area near Tanjong Pagar Police Station; the rubber factory near the junction of Kallang and Geylang Roads; the open area off Paya Lebar Road.

There was fear and trembling in every Chinese home. What did this mean? That was the question on everyone's lips. Even before the decree people were hiding. After the decree, Japanese soldiers with arm-bands of the dread supplementary Kempei went round searching for young Chinese, dragging them into the open spaces. There was no water, and there were no toilets. Here they waited, perhaps for days, to be checked and classified, and given an identification stamp on the shirts, arms or singlets.

The decree, as the Chinese soon discovered, was part of Operation Clean-up. It had been planned by Lieutenant-Colonel Tsuji, officer in charge of planning and action. The 25th Army intended to move to Sumatra. Only the Defence Force would be left behind to hold Singapore. Tsuji argued that before they went the 25th Army should clean up all anti-Japanese elements including the Chinese volunteers who fought so tenaciously against the Japanese, all members of the China Relief Fund, and other anti-Japanese organizations.

Major-General Kawamura, commander of the Defence Force, went to the 25th Army headquarters to question the wisdom of the order, but was told it had been approved by the commander-in-chief, General Yamashita. The clean-up was to be carried out by No. 2 Field Kempei Tai Group to which was seconded an infantry battalion. Members of this battalion acted as supplementary Kempei.

Most of these young soldiers were from the west of Japan—from the countryside: many of them had little more than primary education. They were acting under orders.

Thousands were massacred during this notorious operation. The victims were told the write their names. Some wrote in Chinese, some in English. A knowledge of English at once classified them as pro-British and dangerous. Those with tattoo marks were classified as members of secret societies. Those who failed to apologize at once to the young Kempei for not being able to write their names in Chinese, or for having tattoo marks, were detained and later slaughtered.

Many women came to me for help during this dreadful operation. One Chinese nurse rushed into my hotel one day and tearfully implored me to accompany her to River Valley Road. She had worked in the pre-war Japanese Uemura Clinic.

We drove in my car to this concentration area. There, under the pitiless sun, thousands of Chinese were huddled, each trying to shelter in the shadow of the nearest person. Interrogation of the victims had just started. A young Kempei, with a group of supplementary Kempei and an interpreter, was interrogating a batch of young Chinese. Some were standing, other bowing before the Kempei in fear.

The nurse pointed to her father and brother. They moved towards us. A Kempei stopped them. I told him that these people were employed in a Japanese hospital until the outbreak of war. 'I beg of you to release them.'

'Who are you?' the Kempei shouted angrily.

'Shinozaki, of Defence headquarters,' I replied.

At that he told me to wait while he hurried off to see his commander. Soon an officer came up. I recognized him as Lieutenant Goshi. I had met him when I was released from Changi. We saluted. He said I could take them away with me. 'Their relatives, too?' He nodded. I thanked him and we hurried off.

Simple? Believe me, it required no little guts even for a Japanese in my position to approach the powerful Kempei. I could understand their desire to get away from that concentration area as quickly as they could.

Thousands of eyes watched this incident. I could almost feel their unspoken pleas to me to get them out, too. There was nothing I could do. I stumbled away, sick at my own helplessness.

Another three women were waiting for me at my hotel. Their men were being detained at Jalan Besar. This district was controlled by Lieutenant Onishi, chief of the Kempei Tai Special Branch. My petrol ration came from this unit, so I knew several members of this group personally. Lieutenant Onishi, later Major, had risen from the ranks, and he was by nature a rather sympathetic person. He had already caught several big fish, including Wong Kim Geok, alias Lai Teck, leader of the Malayan Communist Party, and a Chungking spy (he had been trapped by a radio direction finder), and so he was inclined to be comparatively kindly disposed toward the smaller fish. I managed to get the release of the men without much difficulty.

An Eurasian rifle company under Captain Herman de Souza reported to me one day at Toyo Hotel. The captain saluted and explained that his company was a volunteer company. Where should they report? I explained that the Japanese Army was not looking for Malay or Eurasian volunteers. I told him to report to Lieutenant Onishi. I wrote a note to Onishi asking him to release Captain de Souza and his men. Soon the company returned to Toyo Hotel to inform me that Onishi had told them to go home. Later Mr de Souza worked with me in the Education Department.

Bishop Devals came to me for help. We succeeded in collecting a number of Catholics and took them in a bus to a cathedral where they were released.

I was very busy in those days on mercy errands. Sometimes I met stubborn Kempeis. They refused to listen. I was worried about this and went to see Major-General Manaki at Adelphi Hotel. He was already working on the plan for a Japanese military administration for Singapore.

I appealed to him. He confessed he was also worried but Operation Clean-up, he said, was a matter for the 25th Army headquarters and he could not interfere. Yet, as military administrator (and still deputy chief of general staff to General Yamashita), he was very much concerned because the operation could develop into a serious situation which could affect administration.

Eventually he did manage to persuade General Yamashita to allow relatives to bring food and drink to the concentration areas and gradually to release suspects.

Thousands were missing after this tragedy. The fate of

many was never known. Only a few Japanese of high rank knew just how many were massacred.

Meanwhile, I continued to hand out my protection cards, hoping that as many as possible could be rescued from this wall of wire and bayonets.

Later, the Kempei Tai reported that 6,000 Chinese had been killed in Operation Clean-up. It was a crime that sullied the honour of the Japanese Army. About 9,000 civilians were also killed during the fighting and during the bombing and shelling.

4

OVERSEAS CHINESE ASSOCIATION

During Operation Clean-up the Kempei Tai captured lists of members of anti-Japanese organizations. They contained the names of important figures in the China Relief Fund, the Chinese Volunteer Force or Dalforce (named after its leader, Mr Dally, a deputy commissioner of police), and other organizations, including secret societies.

With the discovery of these lists came a new terror. The Kempei Tai began a new wave of arrests. Many influential Chinese leaders were taken into the nearest Kempei Tai branch and detained. The Chinese community lived in fear of a knock at the door, arrest, detention, death.

Indians were protected by the *Fujiwara Kikan* (Organization of the Indian Independence League). At least to begin with, the Japanese treated the Malays well. But war with China still continued; in Singapore the Chinese were therefore treated like enemies.

One day, the Kempei brought to my hotel an old man

with a long white beard. He was Dr Lim Boon Keng, former president of Amoy University. He offered his hand, then staggered. His lips moved but I could hear no words. He seemed to be suffering from shock following his arrest.

The Kempei corporal showed me a newspaper cutting of a picture showing the doctor sitting with a military mission from Chungking. He handed me another piece of paper: it was a letter of thank bearing the stamp of Generalissimo Chiang Kai Shek. 'Look!' exclaimed the corporal excitedly.

Politely I explained to the corporal that I knew this old man very well. Could he leave him with me for a while until Lieutenant-Colonel Yokota returned? I would like to talk to him. The corporal agreed. I took Dr Lim to my room upstairs and ordered Tay Hon Jin to bring us some beer.

I felt I was lucky to have met Dr Lim, for his sake as well as for the sake of others. I told him that the Chinese community was in grave danger. Unless something was done many more could die.

'You, Dr Lim,' I said, 'are among the most respected of Chinese leaders in Singapore. How can we save your people?'

Dr Lim looked at me in some surprise. 'But you are Japanese,' he said.

'True,' I replied. 'But I am not a soldier. I have many friends in China. I have lived in China for four years. I respect Chinese culture—the Chinese are Japan's old teachers. We have learnt many things from China's past. My name means 'Cape of China'. Sino means China and Zaki means Cape. And my first name is Mamoru, which means to protect.' I showed him the Chinese poem I had written in Changi Prison. Dr Lim drank his beer and seemed to be more composed.

Without further delay I explained to him the policy and intention of the Japanese Army. They distrusted the Chinese community; they were suspicious. This had led to persecution and massacres. Operation Clean-up had been followed by arrests. The situation could get worse. Alone, I was powerless. To rescue the Chinese community from their danger I needed the active co-operation of men like himself.

'You ask for my co-operation?' demanded Dr Lim.

I explained to him what was at the back of my mind—the formation of a Chinese organization to co-operate with the Japanese Imperial Army. That would appear on the surface to be the objective. But the real objective would be to protect the Chinese community.

Dr Lim thought it a good idea. How to go about it? I told him he would have to be president of the organization. Dr Lim protested that, at 72, he was too old. His age, educational background, and disinterestedness, I assured him, would be greatly welcomed by the Japanese military authority. I told him that he would not be expected to do much work, just remain as the figurehead.

Eventually he agreed, once he realized that this was an organization intended to protect the interests of the Chinese community.

Dr Lim asked me how old I was. I told him I was 34 and he remarked that I was the same age as his son Peng Hang. This reminded me that his family would be anxious about him. I said I would send him home.

Before I did we agreed that I would approach the military authority about the formation of the organization, ostensibly to co-operate with the Japanese Army. Once the organization had been formed we would submit a list of members in the committee, including all those still under detention by the Kempei Tai. In this way we could make a positive effort to free them.

I suggested that the name of the organization should not be a Peace Maintenance Committee or anything like that. There were organizations like that in China and they were very unpopular, being controlled by military. What was wanted in Singapore was an organization controlled by the Chinese.

Dr Lim agreed and suggested that the name should be Overseas Chinese Association. I thought it was excellent name. Lieutenant-Colonel Yokota returned shortly afterwards. He said that Dr Lim looked much like his own father. The three of us continued our discussions. Yokota approved of the idea, but as a military police officer he was in no position to submit the proposal to higher authorities. He suggested that I should take the matter up with Major-General Manaki, Chief of Administration. I said I would.

I drove Dr Lim home, appointed a young Chinese to be his bodyguard, and provided them both with protection cards—just in case another Kempei should arrest him all over again.

Dr Lim was hiding in a house at River Valley Road. His family was delighted to see him again. Convinced that the formation of the association would protect the Chinese community, Dr Lim declared, 'Now we Chinese are safe.' For me, it was a dramatic moment. I shall never forget it.

Much later, whenever we met to have a drink together, Dr Lim would chuckle about my name. It was a private joke. We got on well together. I called him Papa. He was a clever man, gay and humorous. He sleeps now in his grave in Upper Serangoon Road. His wife died in August 1972 at the age of 88 years.

I had no difficulty in getting the military authority to accept the formation of the Overseas Chinese Association. First I saw Major-General Kawamura. He said it was matter for the Administration, so I should see Major-General Manaki. I told him I already had and that Manaki had told me to consult him first. Kawamura said he had no objections if Manaki had none. So back I went to Adelphi Hotel to see Manaki.

'Right,' he said, 'You had better hurry and get it started.'

I told him that I needed his help to get influential Chinese out of jail into organization. Without these men it would be a spineless organization which would not appeal to the masses of the Chinese community.

Manaki saw the reason of the argument and agreed to consider the list of names if I supplied them, and to talk to the Defence Commander.

I went back to Dr Lim Boon Keng. I showed him the documents I had prepared containing the aims and objects of the Overseas Chinese Association, and the rules. I gave him a list of officials showing Dr Lim as president, Mr S.Q. Wong, vice-president, Mr Robert Tan Hoon Siang, Dr Hu Tsai Kuen and Mr Chen Kee Sun, directors, Mr Tan Yock Soon, secretary, and Mr Chan Kay Chong, assistant secretary.

I submitted this list to the administration. It was approved immediately. Without further delay the Overseas Chinese Association was established in the Chinese Chamber of Commerce building in Hill Street.

Then Mr Tan Yock Soon, Mr Robert Tan, Dr Hu and the others worked hard preparing the list of members. This included some 200 Chinese still in jail. I took the list to Major-General Manaki. Soon afterwards all of them were released. Some were sick and bore the scars and burn-marks of the torture they had undergone. But they were free again, and that, remember, was the real reason for the formation of this association—to save the lives of Chinese.

Not all the Japanese in authority agreed with the association. Lieutenant-Colonel Tsuji and other anti Chinese members of the Army headquarters objected. Soon after it was formed I was told to resign from the organization. I was the adviser. In March 1942 Mr Uchida was appointed as adviser. It was about this time that the Japanese authorities demanded a 'donation' of $50 million from the Chinese community. I was removed from my post as Adviser to Defence headquarters. At Army headquarters I was marked as being pro-Chinese. Major-General Manaki was transferred.

When I was in Saigon after the war to attend a war crimes trial as a witness, I sent Major-General Manaki, then in prison, some cigarettes and toilet paper. I sent them in the name of the Overseas Chinese Association. I believe he appreciated the gesture.

I met Major-General Kawamura in Singapore during his trial at the Victoria Memorial Hall. Before he was hanged in Changi he wrote a book entitled Going Up the 13 Stairs.

In this book he wrote about the organization Dr Lim and I had formed. Unfortunately, many people misunderstood the real aims of the Overseas Chinese Association.

After the $50 million 'donation' had been extracted from the Chinese community, the Overseas Chinese Association was placed under the jurisdiction of the Syonan Tokubetsu Shi. Once again I became the association's adviser.

5

ASSIGNMENT IN SYONAN

On 15 March 1942, Mr Shigeo Odate, formerly of the Japanese Ministry of Home Affairs, arrived in Singapore with some officials from the Ministry. Mr Odate was then a full general. As he walked up the steps of the Municipal Hall wearing a white suit, many thought he was the new civilian mayor of Singapore. In a sense they were right; he was a civilian with the rank of a general. He took orders from the Army.

He came to see me at Toyo Hotel. The cook had prepared a Japanese dinner. During the meal he explained how important it was that the interests of the Singapore Chinese community should be guarded. He said that I understood many of their problems; he urged me to join Tokubetsu Shi—the special City Government. I agreed, no matter what the rank or position. I was given an office on the top floor of the Municipal Building, and from that day until the Japanese surrender there was a never-ending stream of people to see me there.

We instructed all former municipal workers to report for duty. We then set up the various departments. There were few Japanese officials. Most of the appointments were emergency postings. Mr Toyoda, the former consul-general, was appointed deputy mayor. Mr Hosoda of the Japanese Home Affairs Ministry supervised the Public Works Department. Dr Ando was in charge of the Health Department. Mr Furuyama, also of the Japanese Home Affairs Ministry, was in charge of the Police Department. Mr Asahi, an ex-consul, became Custodian of Enemy Property. Finance came under Mr Ogita. I was appointed Head of the Education Department, though I had no previous experience in this field.

My job was to open the schools, and this meant taking many school buildings back from the military. They had been using them as temporary barracks. In addition to this I continued to look after the people's welfare, rescuing all I could from detention, tracing missing persons, giving protection to churches and temples, issuing rice, taking back from the military homes arbitrarily occupied, finding work for the unemployed. I continued issuing protection cards. Later, Mr Nagai, secretary to Mr Toyoda, the deputy mayor, helped to hand out these life-savers.

One day, Mr Tay Tien Swee of the Buddhist Association at Kim Yam Road asked me to try to get Mr Lee Chin Dien released. Lee had been arrested in Sumatra. At the same time, Mr Lim Soo Siam and Mr Chua Hoe Ann had requested me to get Mr Wee Keng Chiang (father of Mr Wee Chou Yaw, former president of the Chinese Chamber of Commerce) out of jail. Wee had been arrested in the Karimoen Islands.

I asked where they were detained and was told they were at the Central Police Station. This was controlled by the military administration of the Kempei Tai. In knew I had a tough job. I did not know this group of Kempei Tai. I set about finding out something about them. The chief I discovered was Lieutenant-Colonel K. Ohtani; his deputy was Lieutenant Mizuma, and the N.C.O. was Sergeant-Major Toyota.

Ohtani was the man responsible for the arrest of the British journalist, Cooks, in Japan. Indirectly, therefore, Ohtani was also responsible for my own arrest, for I was detained by the British in retaliation. I also discovered that Lieutenant Mizuma was born near my hometown in Kyushu.

Armed with this information I decided to call on Ohtani in his office in Fullerton Building.

Entering his office, I saluted and was taken aback when he said, 'So I made you suffer, eh? But you might have been in jail longer but for the speed of our victory.'

Proudly he related the story of how he had arrested Cooks and how Cooks had committed suicide by jumping out of the Tokyo Kempei Tai office on the second floor.

We were discussing my experiences in Changi when we were interrupted by a soldier with an urgent message. Ohtani told me to come back later. I had had no opportunity to bring up the question of the release of Lee and Wee, but at least I had made contact.

I called again the following day and immediately brought up the question of their release. The lieutenant-colonel told me they were directly under the control of Lieutenant Mizuma. 'Ask him. If there are any difficulties come to me.'

I knocked on Lieutenant Mizuma's door. 'Come in!' shouted a voice. Mizuma moved his hand over his bald head. 'What is it? I'm very busy.'

He gave me the impression he was angry. I asked him, very politely, to give special consideration to the question of releasing Wee Keng Chiang and Lee Chin Dien.

He snapped back that they were under strict investigation. He said they were members of the China Relief Fund, and other pro-Chungking groups. Furthermore, they had run away and had hidden themselves. They knew they had done wrong and should be punished. 'I cannot release them,' he said with frightening finality in his voice.

There was silence between us for a moment or two. Then, softly, I asked the lieutenant for the name of his hometown. 'Naogata city,' he replied. I told him I came from Kotake town, very near to Naogata.

At once he was interested to find a Japanese in Singapore from the same district. We chatted amicably for a while, and again I told him why I needed Lee and Wee. I needed these two men, I said, to be directors of the Overseas Chinese Association.

In the end he agreed to go and see Lieutenant-Colonel Ohtani. He came back and said that, provided I took full responsibility for their future behaviour, the two men would be released. 'You must guarantee that,' he said grimly, moving his hand over his bald head.

In the early days when my stamp was sufficient to get the Kempei to release people it was different; these personal negotiations became physically exhausting. It was becoming more and more difficult to persuade the Kempei Tai to let go of their victims. But I continued to try. Months later, when the courts were opened, I petitioned chief judge Sakita for the freedom of Lim Soo Ban. Fortunately, in his case, and in the case of certain others, I was successful. I am sorry I could not do more.

As chief executive of the Education Department, I soon found out that there were few textbooks and many schools were still occupied by the military. We opened the first primary schools in April 1942. I allowed the teaching of English, arithmetic, geography and certain other subjects. The military was annoyed that I had allowed English. I was told the children must learn *Nippon-Go* (Japanese). But there was nothing I could do about that because there were no Japanese teachers, and the first Japanese textbooks did not arrive until July. The teachers came about the same time. However, as the Emperor's birthday approached I concentrated on the Japanese national anthem and pieces of Japanese music.

The administration of Singapore came under the 25th Army headquarters. Reponsible to them were the Malayan and Sumatran military administrations. These organizations controlled the Syonan Tokubetsu Shi and the state governments in Malaya and Sumatra. The military administration set up the *Koa Gaku En* (Asian Institute), which encouraged the teaching of *Nippon-Go*. There was the *Syonan Shian Gakko* (Teachers Training School) where teachers were taught Japanese.

The 25th Army headquarters established the *Koa Kunrensho* (Asia Training School) and the Technical Training School. In Katong, the Japanese Air Force opened their own training school for technicians.

The Synonan Tokubetsu Shi had only four major bureaus: General Affairs, Public Welfare (which included the Education Department), Public Works, and Police.

General Yamashita was strict about ownership of private property and he attached the ex-consul, Mr Asahi, to Army headquarters to handle claims. Mr Asahi set up office in the Supreme Court. He immediately started checking enemy property, including the property of those who had escaped from Singapore: most of these were Chinese. When Mr Asahi returned to Japan his place was taken by Mr Katayama of the Dai-ichi Kangyo Bank Ltd. of Tokyo. Mr Katayama, a banker, was precise and painstaking.

Later, many Singaporeans returning to Syonan lodged claims with the Custodian of Enemy Property for the return of their property and valuables. Most of these claims were successful.

Towards the end of the war, the Japanese authorities in Singapore were tempted to use gold and gems held by the Custodian of Enemy Property. By 1945 the military script (known as banana notes) dropped in value daily. There was little rice. The population of Syonan was more than a million. Money was needed to buy rice from Thailand.

Mayor Naito who succeeded Mayor Odate called a meeting of his senior officials. There it was decided to use jewellery held by the Custodian; certain items of jewellery were, in fact, sent to Bangkok.

But Mr Katayama strongly opposed this and another meeting was held which reversed the decision. Mr Nakata, Director of Economic Affairs, declared, 'If we continue like this we will be labelled as thieves of defeated countries.'

So the jewellery was returned to the Custodian. When the Japanese surrendered, all the enemy property, including the jewellery, was handed over to the British.

The behaviour of the Japanese occupation authorities was not forgotten by some, Mr Aw Boon Haw, for example. When, years after the war, a vicious typhoon laid waste much of northern Kyushu, in Japan, many people lost their homes and property. Deeply touched by the tragedy, Mr Aw sent a cheque for 30 million yen to Japan, through the *Yomiuri Shimbun* (a Japanese newspaper).

In a letter accompanying the cheque, Mr Aw wrote, 'I thought I had lost my valuable collection of jewels during the war, but I was wrong. They had been carefully preserved by the Japanese Custodian of Enemy Property, whom I want to thank. This cheque is a small token of my gratitude. Please distribute it among the victims of the typhoon.'

Mr Katayama read the letter which was reproduced in the newspaper. He felt that it was the finest tribute ever paid to him.

If the Custodian of Enemy Property worked well the same could not be said of all the other government departments during the Japanese occupation. The Syonan Tokubetsu Shi was at the bottom of the administrative structure. In consequence, we had to cope with many difficulties. We were always under pressure. Sometimes we had to protest to Army headquarters, sometimes to military administration.

There were always problems. For example, the chief of the Education and Religious Bureau of the military administration was Lieutenant Ogawa. He had been a professor at Rikkyo University in Tokyo. He was a Protestant and kind-hearted, but he attended only Methodist and Church of England services. He visited and helped only those denominations. This left the other religious organizations dissatisfied and so they came to the Tokubetsu Shi for help.

Sometimes Army headquarters gave orders direct to the City Government without going through military administration. This created unnecessary problems.

Confusion was caused one day when the military administration ordered the Tokubetsu Shi to make official notices henceforth in the Japanese language only. English was forbidden.

Mayor Odate protested to Colonel Watanabe, who succeeded Major-General Manaki as chief of military administration. He explained that most of the population still spoke and read English. To have notices only in Japanese would cause administrative difficulties.

Mayor Odate held the rank of a full general, but he was a civilian officer and, when compared to a military colonel, he was junior to the chief of administration. He could not give orders to the colonel; he could only argue. And this he managed to do successfully. Eventually the order was rescinded.

6
LADY THOMAS

Japanese civil service personnel began to arrive in Singapore almost daily to join the administration staff of the Tokubetsu Shi. Gradually the city began to settle down after the great disrupting storm.

One day, a Chinese nurse ran into my office and said, 'Please come and help Lady Thomas. She is in the military hospital, suffering from dysentery. Japanese soldiers are driving her out. Please hurry.'

Lady Thomas was the wife of Sir Shenton Thomas, the Governor at the fall of Singapore. I stood up immediately. In my room was a case of condensed milk awaiting delivery to a convent. I took this with me and hurried with the nurse to the car and drove at once to the military hospital, now known as Woodbridge Hospital, in Yio Chu Kang.

Kempeis guarded the gate. The young corporal smiled at me. He knew me. When I first met him he was a private. I congratulated him on his promotion.

The Chinese nurse took me to a room where an old lady lay on an uncomfortable-looking bed. The room was part of a suite; there was a room nearby for two British doctors, and there was another room for nurses. The nurse whispered to the old lady. She sat up and held out an emaciated hand. I pressed it gently, and tried to assure her that she could stay there till she had recovered. 'Please,' she said weakly.

I felt near to tears. Here was the former First Lady of Singapore, the heroine of Government House, lying ill on a soldier's iron cot.

Her husband, Sir Shenton, had led the march of the civilians to Changi. Now he was in Taiwan. He had been forced to abandon his sick wife as she was unfit for travel.

I saw the commanding officer of the hospital. He was a surgeon with the rank of lieutenant-colonel. His name was Aoyagi. He agreed to allow Lady Thomas to stay in the hospital until she was well. But, he added, medical units were always on the move. He asked me for a note with my stamp as Lady Thomas' guarantor. This note could be passed to other commanding officers who may follow him. I wrote the note at once.

Lady Thomas was very grateful. I left behind the case of condensed milk and told her that she should get in touch with me if she needed further help. She never did and so I presumed she got well.

Several months later, the new chief of the military hospital told me that Lady Thomas had recovered completely, and was ready to be sent back to the internment camp where she remained until the Japanese surrender. I arranged for an ambulance to take her there.

Before Lady Thomas returned to England at the end of the war she left a message for me. By then I was back in camp, in the internment camp for Japanese civilians at Jurong. I was grateful for her thoughtfulness.

After the war, I heard that Sir Shenton Thomas and Lady Thomas were living in Sussex. Sir Shenton Thomas died in May 1962.

7
GENERAL YAMASHITA

The Japanese love ceremonies, and in Syonan, whenever some significant ceremony was about to take place, I would be approached as Director of Education by the military. Sometimes impetuous young officers at Army headquarters would give me instructions direct instead of going through administration headquarters. The first ceremony was the Emperor's birthday on 29 April.

The Propaganda Department of Army headquarters issued a directive to the Tokubetsu Shi. It said that on the Emperor's birthday the Education Department would organize a march of schoolchildren through the streets of the city. During the march they were to sing the patriotic song, *Aikoku Koshin Kyoku*. Every child was to carry a Japanese flag. The order said that when the commander-in-chief, General Yamashita, appeared on the balcony of City Hall, everyone on the Padang would sing the Japanese national anthem. Then they were to shout *Banzai!* three times. *Banzai* means 'Long live the Emperor'.

It was a hasty decision, for hardly anyone in Singapore knew the Japanese national anthem, and none of the children knew the patriotic song. And there were no copies of the song or the anthem available in Singapore. On top of that we had then not opened the schools. We had not received orders to do so. There were few teachers, no textbooks in Japanese, and much of the furniture was missing—the schools had been looted.

Well, Mr David, chief inspector of English schools, and Mr Lee Chee Hwa, inspector of Chinese schools, began recalling the youngsters back to school. It was about this time that I appointed Mr Herman de Souza, the former captain in the volunteer force and ex-principal of an English school, as an additional inspector of schools. We were in fact operating many schools before the order to do so finally came through.

Another appointment I made was to employ Mr Cordeiro as assistant to Mr de Souza. I first met Mr Cordeiro in Changi Prison. I forgot just why he was there, but I do remember that he was an expert at finding missing things like school pianos, desks, chairs and so forth. He also unearthed large stocks of rice which the British had hidden in rubber estates. I sealed this rice and later used it for the relief of the poor. I delivered stocks to temples and churches and other charitable organizations. I followed his pattern when I later became in charge of the distribution of rice, sugar and salt. Cordeiro was later transferred to the Naval Base because parents discovered that an ex-convict was working for the Education Department and protested in anxiety for their children.

Neither de Souza, Cordeiro nor I could lay our hands on a single sheet of Japanese music, let alone the patriotic song and the national anthem. Fortunately for me and the Emperor's birthday celebrations, I managed to find a soldier who had been a music teacher in Japan. He wrote the music of the patriotic song and the national anthem. Once I had copies made, I gathered all the music teachers. They mastered the two songs within an hour. Then they rushed back to their schools. Every day from then on the schoolchildren rehearsed the songs.

Shortly before the Emperor's birthday I arranged a mass rehearsal on the green in Bras Basah Road. Thousands of children sang to the music of the police band. Hundreds of Japanese soldiers joined in.

For the Emperor's birthday, we divided the schoolchildren into two groups—those from the east of Orchard Road and those coming from the west. We planned that the two groups would link up in front of the Municipal building.

Precisely at ten o' clock that morning, General Yamashita stepped out on to the balcony. He was accompanied by his A.D.C. and chief of staff, General Suzuki (later to be killed in action at Lyete, in the Philippines, in 1944), and Mayor Odate. The adjutant and I stood behind them with the deputy mayor, Mr Toyoda, and several others.

I hoped the children would do well. There was good reason for my anxiety: I was the programme director for the day, and the Japanese took their ceremonies seriously.

At first General Yamashita stood with his hands behind his back. His pot-belly protruded a bit, but he looked dignified.

Gradually the sound of the police band became louder. Then we could hear the voices of the children singing. It sounded grand: the tune was correct and the timing superb. They were singing *Aikoku Koshin Kyoku*—Look at the dawn over the Eastern Seas.

Impressed, General Yamashita moved to the front of the balcony to get a better look at the children. Then we could see them, row after row of them. They stopped in front of the main steps of the building, flags in their hands.

I looked at the general. There were tears in his eyes. Then the children sang the Japanese national anthem. here was silence for a moment, then they shouted *Banzai!* three times. Every Japanese, including myself, felt very happy. The general turned to me and whispered, 'Just like Japanese children, aren't they?' He saluted the children several times.

General Yamashita made no attempt to hide his emotion—tears ran down the face of this man they called the Tiger of Malaya. Most of those children who stood so correctly that day on the Padang and sang so well must now be over 40 years old. How many of them, I wonder, remember that occasion?

As soon as the children marched off, General Yamashita and his group moved to the Adelphi Hotel, almost next door. I had to get there before him, for I was director of that affair as well. The general was to meet hundreds of Singaporeans there. While we waited for the general to arrive, a Hungarian orchestra practised some Japanese music. When Yamashita walked in they began to play Aikoku Koshin Kyoku. He saluted the people as he walked to the platform at the end of the room and they bowed to him. They clapped politely.

'Today,' Yamashita told them, 'we celebrate the Emperor's birthday with you. You have just become our new subjects. It is my great pleasure to be with you on this auspicious day. I want the people of Malaya and Sumatra to carry on with their affairs, for they are now our new subject people.'

When I heard the general talking about 'our subject people' I thought that he must have already received the approval of Tokyo to say this. But apparently he had not. And he was to pay dearly for his mistake.

Japanese reporters cabled his remarks back to their newspapers and Tokyo's reaction was that General Yamashita had made a political blunder.

Not long afterwards, Field-Marshal Terauchi, the supreme commander of the Japanese forces in Southeast Asia, came to Singapore from Saigon. He stayed at the Istana, formerly Government House.

It was at the Istana that Field-Marshal Terauchi conveyed to General Yamashita his orders from General Tojo. General Yamashita was ordered to proceed direct to Northere Manchuria from Syonan. He was not to visit Tokyo.

This order deprived General Yamashita, victor of Malaya, of the opportunity of seeing the Emperor, an honour the general would have valued highly.

There were many reasons for this slap in the face. Tojo was known to dislike Yamashita and to be quite jealous of him. And Yamashita's speech had caused displeasure in Tokyo. And so, after the $50 million 'donation' from the

Chinese community had been collected, General Yamashita left Syonan for Manchuria.

I expect many Singaporeans can still remember that first Emperor's birthday celebrations. There was a concert at Victoria Memorial Hall, Japanese music played by the Hungarian orchestra, and a Japanese opera by a troupe from Shanghai.

As part of these celebrations the Army ordered community leaders to make speeches at the Cathay Cinema. Dr Paglar was one of the speakers. He was president of the Japanese-organized Eurasian Welfare Association. When the British military administration took over after the Japanese surrender, Dr Paglar was prosecuted by the British, but the charges were dropped.

8
$50 MILLION DONATION

If the Japanese authorities wanted to win the Chinese community in Singapore over to their side they made a great mistake in forcing them to make a $50 million 'donation', especially since the Japanese insisted upon calling it a voluntary 'gift'.

I have already explained that while Major-General Manaki, Singapore's first military administrator, did not want the newly formed Overseas Chinese Association to be rigidly controlled by the military, his view was not shared by Colonel Watanabe, his successor.

Colonel Watanabe decided to make the fullest possible use of the Overseas Chinese Association. First he got rid of me as adviser. My place was taken by Mr Uchida. Mr Wee Twee Kim, a Taiwanese, was attached to the association as an interpreter.

It was about this time that Mr Takase, who was Colonel Watanabe's own adviser, arrived in Syonan. Takase and

Watanabe had known each other for a long time. They had both served in China, and Takase never let anyone forget it.

Mr Takase considered himself an orator, and whenever new civil service officials arrived from Japan, he would greet them with speeches during which he stressed the New China policy. He openly advocated brutality, which he called realism, and urged officials to reject humanism and humane attitudes during war.

He criticized my own policy of reasonableness towards to the Chinese community. I had no set policy other than that. Sometimes I would be questioned by the Japanese about my policy. I would tell them that I had no set policy: my reactions and attitudes varied from case to case. If I had an outline of a policy it was based on sympathy and consideration for the weak. Some Japanese would remark that this did not make me a very suitable man to employ during wartime.

Mr Takase claimed to be a Confucian, as well as an authority on China and all things Chinese. He based this claim upon his stay in China and Manchuria. He mistakenly assumed that the Chinese community in Singapore behaved like the Chinese in China and observed the same customs. He wanted to rule with force backed by Confucian guidelines. What he failed to understand was that many Chinese in Singapore were born in Singapore, had been educated in English language schools, and could not read or write Chinese characters. They knew little about Confucius.

Mr Takase began enthusiastically to collect the $50 million 'donation'. He summoned the Chinese community leaders, including those released from the Kempei Tai cells. He called a meeting at Wu Loo Club. Mr Lo Tien Po, liaison officer for the Overseas Chinese Association, was instructed to be responsible personally for the collection, and, understandably, he made many enemies. After the war he left Singapore to live in Hong Kong.

Although I had been ordered to sever my connection with the association, I did all I could to help the victims and submitted petitions and pleas to Mr Lo on behalf of those in difficult circumstances. Takase had instructed that all property owners must contribute eight per cent of the value of the property. Some of these people owned property but had no money. Among them were women whose husbands were missing. They were called upon to 'donate' in the names of their husbands.

There was little cash about and the banks were still closed. When the Singapore banks did open they had to use notes supplied by the Yokohama Specie Bank. Of the $50 million, Singapore had to raise $10 million and Malaya the rest. Singapore did manage to raise their $10 million, but all that Malaya could collect was $18 million. And so, on their behalf, the military administration borrowed the balance of $22 million from the Yokohama Specie Bank.

Takase and Wee Twee Kim threatened the Chinese community leaders, saying that the Japanese Army wanted to kill every Chinese. They must pay up to save their lives. To add to Mr Lo's troubles Wee would lay some of the blame for their unhappiness on him. I heard many tragic stories of husbands being arrested and wives tortured to reveal the allegedly hidden family fortunes.

Many more people came to me to intervene with Mr Lo. I became a thorn in the flesh of the military administration.

I was eventually summoned by the mayor. He told me he was sending me to Japan for a holiday. 'But don't go in an Army plane. You have friends in the Navy—go in a Navy plane.' So I went round to the Naval Liaison Office (in the Goodwood Park Hotel) and on 11 June 1942 flew to Tokyo. Without delay I went to see the Foreign Minister, Togo, and offered my resignation. But two months later I returned to Singapore. There was a new military administrator, and the Overseas Chinese Association had been transferred back to the City Government. I again became adviser. Uchida and Takase were back in Japan, and Wee Twee Kim was no longer employed by the authorities. After the war, I was told that he had been killed by anti-Japanese forces.

There is no doubt that the $50 million 'donation' scheme caused a great deal of misery. Unfortunately some of the Chinese community blamed the leaders of the Overseas Chinese Association for starting it. This was not true, but once the Japanese had started the collection, the community leaders were forced to help. They had no alternative if they wanted to live.

In the course Syonan became the headquarters for the Japanese Southern Area Command. Field-Marshal Terauchi resided at Government House. Superfically, Syonan appeared to be peaceful. Major-General Nishijoo took over as military administrator from Colonel Watanabe, but he was soon replaced by Major-General Fujimura. Both these generals were much more reasonable and judicious than Colonel Watanabe, and neither made any attempt to follow Watanabe's anti-Chinese policy.

The balance of the loan of $22 million owed to the Yokohama Specie Bank was never paid. Solemnly, Mr Muto, the manager of the back, told me after the Japanese surrender that this would be cancelled!

At Army Headquarters on the Emperor of Japan's birthday in 1942.
General Yamashita (left), Marquis Tokugawa (centre) and the Sultan of
Johore in a conversation.

Left: Marshal Terauchi, Supreme Commander of the Japanese Southern Regions, 1942.

Right: Major-General Kawamura, Commander of the Syonan Defence Force.

Above: Dr Lim Boon Keng, 1942.

Below: The $50 million 'donation' paid by the Overseas Chinese Association.

9

JAPANESE INFLUX

For some time after the first Emperor's birthday celebrations there were no Japanese textbooks in the schools. Most of the class-time was in consequence devoted to singing and physical exercise.

Syonan had become the regional Japanese military supply base, and many Japanese firms had opened branches in order to supply the military quickly. Some dealt with the Military Supply Corporation, some with the Vehicle Corps, or the Sea Transport Corps, the Air Force, Naval Construction, etc. All this meant a considerable influx of Japanese civilians for whom accommodation had to be found. Companies also needed factory space.

Some Japanese went about acquiring houses and factories properly, leasing them from their owners; others misbehaved, and soon I was issuing Singaporeans with protection cards for their homes instead of for themselves.

Nippon Chisso Co. Ltd., for example, wanted to take

over the Ho Hong Oil Mill in Havelock Road. Mr Lim Peng Mao, chairman of the company, came to me for protection. We went to see the mayor. He authorized me to settle the matter. I called the managers of Nippon Chisso and Ho Hong Oil Mill together and we worked out a three-year agreement. Nippon Chisso would lease the factory on a monthly rental basis and employees of the mill were guaranteed employment at the previous rates. There were several similar cases, including the Johore Pineapple Factory.

Then there was the Japanese *ryotei* which was set up in Nan Hua Chinese Girls High School in Sophia Road by the owners of one of Japan's famous *ryotei* in Tokyo. A Japanese *ryotei* is a restaurant, bar and inn where liquor is served, and *geishas* provide musical and other entertainment. This *ryotei* was established in the school with the support of a senior Army staff officer. The entire building was furnished in Japanese style, complete with *tatami* mats on the floor, Japanese waitresses and *geishas*. Every night the hoarse voices of Japanese officers could be heard raised in song, disturbing nearby residents.

Following complaints, the mayor asked me to contact the owner of the *ryotei* (which was called *Kaniya*) to tell him that the school was needed for its original purpose.

I went along to see him. He was as giant of a man, weighing well over 230 pounds. He had a big scar on his face. He became very angry when I told him I wanted the building that was a girls' school. He said he was sorry about that, but he could not give up the premises. And I could not force him to do so, he said, because he had the powerful support of the Army.

He did have that for a while, and then All-India Radio began to broadcast from New Delhi stories about the Japanese using the girls' school as a *ryotei*. The top brass in the Army checked, found this was so and ordered the *ryotei* to be closed.

Takase, Colonel Watanabe's declamatory adviser, and the man principally responsible for the infamous $50 million 'donation', set up a Japanese inn in the Singapore Cricket Club. He furnished this *Yamato Butai* in the Japanese style most lavishly. It became the most luxurious restaurant and bar for officials of the military administration. There were many girls, some from Japan. Officially they were called typists and clerks. But they were much more, most of them. Every afternoon the noisy laughter of these girls could be heard in the mayor's office in City Hall, a couple of hundred yards away.

Field-Marshal Terauchi was still in Syonan at this time. Now and then he invited the mayor to Government House for a game of go, or stone chess. During a game on one occasion the mayor casually asked him why he did not raid the Yamato Butai. The Field-Marshal said he had never heard of the place. What is it? The mayor told him in some detail. Shortly afterwards the Yamato Butai was closed. Those girls who were genuine typists were allowed to remain; they became office workers. The rest returned to Japan.

It was in early April 1942 that the Japanese fleet, under Admiral Nakumo, that had attacked Pearl Harbour and later sunk the British aircraft carrier Hermes off Ceylon, entered Singapore. Admiral Nakumo's fleet, including the battleships *Haruna, Kongo* and *Hiei* (each 32,000 tons), the aircraft carriers *Kaga, Akagi, Hiryu* and *Soryu*, and a heavy cruiser, some light cruisers, destroyers and submarines, numbered sixty vessels.

This fleet was joined by the Southern Squadron led by Admiral Ozawa. The mighty Japanese armada completely filled the Singapore seafront with an impressive silhouette, the like of which had never been seen before, and might never be seen again.

Naval officers and ratings swarmed into Syonan. One of my naval friends stationed in Singapore invited me to the Tsukushi, now the American Club, to meet some of the officers from the ships in the harbour. He told me, 'We'll draw out the American fleet to Midway. And there we will attack them and completely destroy them.'

Nobody could have foreseen the shattering blow this great fleet was to receive at the hands of the Americans at Midway a few weeks later. What actually happened was that the Japanese fleet lost four aircraft carriers and one heavy cruiser at Midway. Perhaps a greater loss were 200 fighter pilots.

I had many friends in the Navy and was often invited to Seletar Naval Base to lecture. Captain Shigematsu of the warship *Kashii* often came to my home in Cavenagh Road with his men, and on many occasions we would drink in the garden until midnight. Indeed, whenever a Japanese warship visited Seletar my place would soon begin to look like a naval club. I remember that the commander of the Seletar Naval Air Force was Captain Furuta. We called him General Chiang Kai Shek because of his remarkable resemblance to the generalissimo.

Captain Shigematsu was transferred to the battleship *Haruna* which fought at the battle on the Solomon Sea. He sank an American warship. Captain Furuta told me that as soon as Captain Shigematsu saw that the American ship was mortally hit and that the sailors were jumping into the sea, he ordered his gunnery officer to stop firing and deliberately turned away to allow other American ships to rescue them.

Captain Shigematsu died in the second battle on the Solomon Sea. Captain Furuta who told me all this died in action himself soon afterwards. I found most of the Japanese naval officers to be gentlemen.

Syonan had changed much during my two months' stay in Tokyo. The Japanese community had grown, there were many more Japanese companies, and the City Government was staffed with a greater number of Japanese officials. Mr Dazai was now head of the Education Department and he worked closely with a group of Japanese teachers who had arrived with Japanese textbooks.

Qualified Japanese engineers and technicians were in charge of public utilities; the British engineers and technicians were in the prisoner of war camps.

Japanese repatriates began to come from India; and from Japan came a number of former Japanese residents of Singapore. They came to Syonan full of optimism, but they were quickly disappointed, for the controls exercised by the military administration continued to be strict. They were not permitted to reopen their old pre-war businesses. Instead, they were all seconded to the military administration.

I was welcomed back by the Chinese community leaders—Yuan Yeck Lin, S.Q. Wong, Chen Kee Sun, and

Leong Yuen Ho, among others. Here, in Syonan, I found a country capable of arousing in me the sort of warmth and love that I could find I in the land of my birth. Strangely, I felt my heart turning away from my own people because as a group they were becoming more arrogant and proud.

The Japanese newcomers did not know what had happened in Singapore at the beginning of the occupation. They had no idea how frightfully the Chinese community had suffered. They were inclined to look upon this chap Shinozaki as being too pro-Chinese.

I had been appointed head of the Welfare Department (*Kosei-Ka*), and the very nature of my job put me in a position whereby I had to stand by the people of Singapore against the official and unofficial pressure of the Japanese occupation authorities. Many Japanese hated me for this.

Soon after my return from Japan, the deputy mayor, Mr Toyoda, told me to look after members of Singapore's pre-war Japanese community returning from Japan. It was a painful and thankless task to tell them about conditions in Syonan, and to inform them that the military authorities would not permit Japanese to run individual businesses. Those of military age would be drafted to become interpreters or to do other work in the military administration.

I met the boat and told them all this. It was particularly distressing for me because among them were several old friends. I boarded the ship as soon as she entered Keppel Harbour. Everyone was on deck. They had Japanese flags in their hands. They had high hopes and I had to destroy the plans they had made. Some were sad as I spoke, others were angry. There were 200 of them. I took them for a short tour in buses. Our first stop was at Mount Faber where the Japanese 18th Division had fought the final battle for Singapore; then on to Bukit Timah, where General Yamashita had accepted General Percival's surrender. Our final destination was the Japanese school in Waterloo Street which was to be their temporary home. They did not like that very much, but there were no hotels available. They stayed in the school for some time.

Towards the end of August 1942, the first batch of Japanese who had been interned in India returned to Syonan in the prisoner of war exchange ship, the *Tatsutu Maru*. We had to quarter them in the Japanese school in Waterloo Street as well. The younger ones had to join the military administration of the City Government, but there were many old Japanese among them whom nobody wanted. They were left with their bitter thoughts.

It was about this time that the Commerce and Industry Department and Food Supply Department of the City Government decided to form an agency to facilitate the distribution of essential commodities. The agency was called the Singapore Commodities Distribution Union (*Syonan Busshi Haikyu Kumiai*). And this is where we managed to find work for the older Japanese. They helped organize the daily deliveries of commodities such as rice, sugar, textiles, etc., to the people from the City Government. Mr Sugiyama, the former president of the Nanyang Shoko Ltd., was elected chairman of the Distribution Union. A number of Singaporeans worked under the Japanese directors, some of whom spoke Malay fluently and knew the markets well. I believe that this Distribution Union was probably the best-run organization in Syonan during the Japanese occupation. Japanese businessmen who wanted to run their own businesses were strongly opposed by the Union and by myself. Mr N. Shimoda, president of the Shimoda Trading Company, was among the leaders of this group.

I recall him arriving one day at a luncheon organized by the Distribution Union to celebrate its inauguration. He was late and the worse for liquor. In a loud voice he criticized the military administration and the City Government for what he considered to be the ill-treatment of the former Japanese residents of Singapore. Everyone knew that Shimoda had been refused permission to re-establish his company in Syonan, at least for the time being.

Shimoda came over to me and openly accused me of doing too much for the Chinese, 'our enemies'. He spoke of the suffering the Japanese had endured in India. 'Now we must take our revenge, but you are protecting them!' he shouted.

He kept on abusing me, till finally I lost my temper and knocked him down. Dr Ishida grabbed hold of me from behind. Shimoda left the hall. Soon afterwards he went back to Japan. He remained, until his death in Kyoto some ten years ago, one of my most severe detractors.

It was the Distribution Union that kept the commodities moving in the Japanese internment and prisoner of war camps in Jurong after the Japanese surrendered. The same Japanese kept the system working, then in their own interests as much as in the interests of others.

10
MILITARY ADMINISTRATION

There were many bosses in Syonan. At the top of them all was the Supreme Command of the Southern army headquarters. Then came the 25th Army headquarters, the Defence headquarters, the Air Force headquarters, Sea Transport Corps, the Navy, Supply Corps, Vehicle Corps and several others. Later, the 25th Army went to Sumatra and the 29th Army took over.

Then came the military administration department, and under this department were the Malay military administration headquarters and the City Government (*Tokubetsu Shi*).

What created considerable confusion was that nearly all the bosses issued orders or made requests to the Tokubetsu Shi, usually disregarding the lines of command. There were, for instance, many experts from the Japanese Ministry of Home Affairs. They issued a stream of notices, laws, regulations concerning supplies, prices, changes in pattern of trade, free labour services, taxes on luxury goods, the confiscation of gold and jewellery, the prohibition of the removal of important material, and the prohibition on listening to foreign broadcasts.

The last one was a very important regulation rigorously enforced. Anybody caught listening to overseas broadcasts was immediately arrested by the Kempei Tai. Some were executed after trial—decapitated.

Every day the newspapers devoted at least one page to official notices. I held a 'meet-the-people' session every week, on Sunday, to explain what they meant. A friend whispered to me, 'You Japanese are legalized bandits.'

American submarines were now attacking and sinking Japanese transport ships in convoys and in single raids. Supplies of all commodities were becoming scarcer and scarcer. The police issued rice cards for every family.

These cards authorized a ration of eight katis per person per month (half for children) from the Distribution Union. Besides rice, the Union distributed cigarettes, matches, salt, sugar, textiles and other necessities besides cooking oil. The rice ration was cut to six katis in early 1944.

Inevitably a black market thrived. Towards the end of war a tin of State Express cigarettes cost $5000, a sheet of corrugated iron cost $1300, a bag of cement $1300, a yard of cloth between $300 and $400, woollens $1500 a yard. A tin of butter would fetch $950, a case of powdered milk, $25,000.

Who operated the black markets? Lots of people, including retired government servants, people who disliked working under the Japanese, former bankers and newspapermen. Extra rice given to a person working for the military usually went into the black market where it was worth $6 or $7 a kati.

One pleasant recollection of the Japanese occupation is the reasonably-priced and very tasty Kirin beer. This was brewed by the Kirin Beer Kaisha on the premises of Tiger Brewery, off Alexandra Road. Mr Takeishi and Mr Nakamura were responsible for this beer. They are still connected with Kirin Beer in Japan. They are both senior executives of the company.

In Syonan there were also a number of imitation foods, as well as strong drink such as tapioca brandy and Nanboku whisky. Some people soused on the brandy were said to have woken up blind, but I used to drink Nanboku whisky and found it very good at that time.

Not that there was much drinking among the people during the occupation. There was very little entertainment of any kind, no enjoyment. All the main theatres were reserved exclusively for Japanese soldiers. Unnecessarily, Singapore people were shut out of most luxurious bars and restaurants. Even if had they been open to them few could have afforded to have gone inside; they did not have the money.

One day, Professor Nakajima of Tokyo University, accompanied by Mr G.H. Kiat, came into my office and suggested that we form a sports association. I promptly agreed and so the Syonan Sports Association came into being. Lots of youngsters joined; we used the Jalan Besar Stadium. This was in fact the only institution in Syonan where everybody was treated equally. Japanese, Malays, Chinese, Indians, Eurasians, Arabs—all were on exactly the same footing. Many lifetime friendships were started in this association. Mr T.S. Khoo (the *Domei* news reporter, now chief editor of *The Straits Times*) was an active committee member.

Games were played between the races—a Chinese team for example might play a mixed races team, or a Malay team or a Japanese team. There were boxing matches as well as soccer and basketball. Mr Goh Chye Hin and Mr Loh Ah Fong often officiated as referees. Sometimes Lieutenant Okamoto of the military administration helped out as a referee. Singapore teams went to Seremban, Kuala Lumpur, Malacca, Ipoh and Penang. Boxing tournaments were held at the Great World in aid of charity.

As the months passed, life in Syonan became more difficult. For many it became a struggle for survival. Probably the man with the most difficult job was the Controller of Food.

Most of the food came from Thailand in lorries, in trains and in ships. But there was never enough to fill the bellies of a million hungry people.

Food shortage changed the appearance of the city as much as that of the people. Tapioca and sweet potato plants replaced flowering plants in practically every garden, every patch of available land. The city authorities closed their eyes to the black market—at least some food was available for those who could afford it.

The black market is a curious phenomenon; in times of stress it operates everywhere, in Europe and in the United States as well as in the communist countries. The Japanese military administration in Syonan could not stamp out the black market, and so they too went to the black market to buy what they needed.

Of course the city administration tried to control the situation: they made changes in the trade laws; there were taxes on luxuries, there was a law prohibiting the removal of important machinery, boats and cars; there were regulation on savings, the promotion of self-sufficiency state lotteries, taxation, price control, licence fees, gambling farms—but all to no avail. The black market thrived, as it did elsewhere in the world.

A short supply of commodities encouraged invention and there were many Japanese technicians, engineers and chemists in Singapore. They invented many things, using Singapore products and materials, and some new industries where thus created. I believe that this experience partly helped to develop industrial Japan after the war.

Did the people of Singapore benefit from their terrible experience during the Japanese occupation? I believe they did in some ways. The people of Singapore proved they could look after themselves in adversity. They produced shark-liver oil, they ran a taxi service with taxis operating on charcoal. Singapore paper and Chinese sauces were made.

I think the Japanese occupation was probably a historical necessity in Singapore's political and subsequent economic development.

Life for me was not very pleasant. For example, when I went to the Kempei Tai to ask them to release Mr S.Q. Wong's car I was accused of being an enemy of Japan.

The Kempei Tai headquarters was in the Y.M.C.A building. The man in charge of the case was a warrant officer. He was tall and fat, with a big round face. He was arrogant. I explained to him that Mr Wong was the vice-president of the

Overseas Chinese Association. This was a most important society and was respected by the City Government.

He wanted until I had finished then he shouted, 'Are you a Chinese or a Japanese? The Chinese must be paying you.'

I was shocked. I told him it was my duty to protect civilians. I worked with sincerity and in good faith. I was not interested in money.

'Duty! Faith! You are a cheeky fellow. Hi! *Toban!* (soldier on duty) Lock him up in a cell.'

The young Kempei soldier, recognizing me, took me instead to Sub-Lieutenant Takenaka. He understood what I was trying to do. He told me that Mr Wong's big car had already been delivered to General Headquarters. There was nothing he could do about that car but he could offer me another, a small Ford. I thanked him and took it, then handed it over to Mr P.T. Wong, the son of Mr S.Q. Wong.

I came out of the Y.M.C.A. Kempei Tai that day hot and angry, still smarting from the insults of the warrant officer. If I tried to help the Chinese I must be an enemy because, he argued, the Chinese were the enemies of Japan. What was frightening was that many Japanese soldiers thought like this warrant officer. Looking after the welfare of the people of Singapore, most of whom were Chinese, in these circumstances presented enormous difficulties.

I felt sad, lonely and dispirited until I reminded myself that the lot of Singapore people was far worse than mine.

11
INDIAN INDEPENDENCE LEAGUE

Three months before the war started, in September 1941, Major Fujiwara, an Imperial Army headquarters staff officer, formed the Southern Intelligence Corps. From the Nakano School (Army Intelligence Centre), and from among graduates of Tokyo's College of Foreign Studies and Kobe University, he carefully selected his staff. They were put through an intensive officers' training course. They were then sent to Bangkok under false names. They pretended to be company clerks.

Their real work was to keep in close contact with the Indian Independence League movement. Later they came to Malaya. They spoke fluent Malay, Cantonese and Hokkien. Some infiltrated into Singapore as photographers, many as clerks. And here they waited for the Japanese invasion. Their code name was F. Kikan.

India's independence was declared by the Independence League at Haadyai, near the Malayan border, by Mr Pritam Singh on 10 December 1942.

Later, Captain Mohan Singh of the 11th Indian Division was captured by the Japanese on a Malayan battlefront. He was approached by Lieutenant Kunizuka of F. Kikan with a proposal that they should co-operate to achieve India's independence. The two men got on well together and soon became friends. Captain Mohan Singh persuaded many men under his command to defect to the Japanese Army. Other Indian units were also approached. This movement snow-balled until a large number of Indian troops of the 11th Indian Division began to lay down their arms. This brought about a series of retreats by the British down the Malay Peninsula.

F. Kikan also captured Tunku Abdul Rahman (later to become Malaysia's first Prime Minister). They promised his father, the Sultan of Kedah, to protect the Malays. It was as a result of this pledge to the Sultan, and the agreement between F. Kikan and the leaders of the Indian Independence League, that most Malays and Indians were not bullied or ill-treated during the Japanese occupation.

After the fall of Singapore, F. Kikan urged the Indian community to join the Indian Independence League. In May 1942, Mr Subhas Chandra Bose came to Syonan from Tokyo. Mr Bose became the president of the League.

The first mass meeting of overseas Indians was held in Bangkok. There was a resolution passed to organize Indians the world over into a gigantic Indian Independence movement centred in Singapore.

Mass meetings were held in Singapore at Farrer Park, sometimes with as many as 30,000 people attending. The meetings were addressed by Mr Bose, Mr Pritam Singh and

Lieutenant Kunizuka. The Indians were great orators. The Japanese lieutenant spoke in English.

Most of the league members were Hindus. Many Muslime Indians refused to join. Mr Anwari, in fact, opposed the league. He came to me and suggested the formation of an Indian Welfare Association. This presented a problem because the city authorities could not oppose the might of F. Kikan. So we had to tell Mr Anwari that we would keep his proposal in mind.

Much later approval was given for the formation of a Malay Welfare Association, a Eurasian Welfare Association, and Arab Welfare Association and an Indian Welfare Association entirely devoid of any political interest. These associations were formed as a liaison bridge between the communities and the city authorities. Dr Nathan was appointed president of the Indian Welfare Association. Mr Anwari was detained until the end of the war. There was, unfortunately, nothing I could do to help him.

Much, much later, F. Kikan was replaced by the Iwakuro Kikan. Major Fujiwara returned to Japan. His place was taken by Colonel Iwakuro.

Mr Chandra Bose was an interesting man. He has been a political refugee in Germany. He had been smuggled to Germany from his home in Calcutta (where he was under house arrest) by a submarine which had waited for him at the mouth of the Hooghly River. Then he moved to Tokyo.

In July 1943, Mr Subhas Chandra Bose addressed a packed meeting at the Cathay Cinema. With him was Mr Rash Behari Bose. The audience consisted of Indians living in many countries.

In many ways, Subhas Bose was a brilliant individual. At this meeting, he was made president of the Provisional Government of India and Supreme Commander of the Indian National Army. Until then, Captain Mohan Singh had been the commander of the Indian National Army.

On 6 July 1943, General Tojo, the Japanese Premier, came to Syonan to inspect the Indian National Army. A parade was held on the Padang. General Tojo and his A.D.C. were on the balcony of the City Hall with Mr Subhas Bose, Colonel Iwakuro and a group of senior officers of the Indian National Army. On parade were light tanks, gun-tractors and troops. The troops carried British weapons; the light tanks and gun-tractors were Japanese.

Mighty, lusty shouts of 'On to Delhi! *Azad Hind*!' filled the air. Every Indian that day in Syonan was wildly excited. I am sure they would that day have all been prepared to die for India. There were Indian flags everywhere.

Unexpectedly I had, shortly before General Tojo's arrival in Singapore, received an order from Army headquarters. Japan's Premier, I was told, wished to see a cross-section of the people of Syonan. I was instructed to get together as many leaders of each community as I could and assemble them in front of City Hall.

I instantly relayed the order to the various community associations including the Overseas Chinese Association. I was relieved to see that they all turned up in large numbers. Boards were held aloft bearing the name of each community. I stood beside the bearded Dr Lim Boon Keng, president of the Overseas Chinese Association.

After the parade of the Indian National Army was over,

General Tojo hurriedly walked down the steps and came straight to us.

'Who is this old man?' he asked briskly.

I told him. He saluted Dr Lim, then hurried to his car which was flying the flag of Japan's supreme general. As suddenly as he arrived, he left—like a whirlwind. He left behind 20,000 of us very tired from the long hours spent on the Padang.

Before he took off for Tokyo, General Tojo gave us a gift of a large sum of money. Deputy Mayor Toyoda suggested we should spend it on a dinner for the community leaders who had helped to organize the parade. I invited about 120 of them to the Nanmei Soo, the former Dutch Club, the next day. There were speeches. In spite of the presence of two Kempei Tai personnel I made a rather emotional address. I spoke in English. I urged them to understand why the military pressed them so hard. Forgive my countrymen, I asked. I told them I knew of the people's suffering. I promised to continue to do what I could for them.

Soon the strength of the Indian National Army was reported to be 80,000. Actually the figure was 30,000 and this included thousands of Indian boys and girls.

On 24 October 1943, Japan, Wang Chin Wei's China, the Philippines, Thailand, Manchukuo, Germany and Italy recognized the Provisional Government of India, which declared war against Britain and the United States.

Young mothers with babies in their arms drilled daily with young office girls, shop assistants and other Indians in Bras Basah Road. When the instructors called intervals the young mothers breast-fed their infants. A well-known lady,

Dr S. Lakshmi, was appointed the head of this regiment of determined women which was called the Ranee of Jhansi Regiment. Soon their ranks were joined by volunteers from Malaya and Thailand.

Beautiful, talented, well-educated Dr Lakshmi became a firm friend of Miss M. Ohmori, secretary of the Marquis Tokugawa, then the director of the Singapore Museum. Often I saw these two women walking along Stamford Road and, like many others, was struck by their beauty and grace.

Early in 1944 the Indian National Army, including elements of the Ranee of Jhansi Regiment, moved to Burma, and then to Kohima near the Indian frontier. But the British under General William Slim were fighting back, and at Imphal defeated the Japanese Army. This was the first major setback suffered by the hitherto all-conquering Japanese Army. The Indian National Army was also severely mauled. After Imphal nothing more was heard of the Ranee of Jhansi Regiment, or its attractive leader, Dr Lakshmi. This flower of Indian independence disappeared forever. I have often wondered what happened to her. Neither she nor her determined band of women deserve to be forgotten.

When Mr Bose returned from Burma he asked me to call and see him at his residence at Katong. This was in late May 1945. With him were Lieutenant-Colonel A.C. Chatterji, Lieutenant-Colonel Yamamoto of the Japanese Army, and several officers of the Indian National Army. Without any preliminaries, Mr Bose requested me to hand over the administration of the Indian Welfare Association to his army. This, as I explained to Mr Bose, was not easy. The Welfare Association had been formed by Indians in

Syonan to look after their interests. Many of the leaders of the Indian community in Syonan felt that the Welfare Association served a useful purpose by acting as a liaison body between the Indian community and the city authorities.

Mr Bose seemed to understand this, but not Yamamoto. He became intensely angry and Lieutenant-Colonel Chatterji had to calm him down before I could leave the room.

Mr Bose died in an aircraft accident in Taipeh on 18 August 1945. The plane had just taken off for the Soviet Union. Mr Bose was severely burnt. He died six hours later in the military hospital in Taipeh. His ashes were taken to Rengoji Temple in Tokyo by his A.D.C. Colonel Habib Ur Rehman. It was reported at the time that Lieutenant-Colonel Chatterji was in the plane when it crashed. The report said that there was a lot of jewellery with them. No trace of this was ever found.

During the occupation a monument to the memory of those in the Indian National Army who fell in battle, or in active service, was erected in a corner of the Padang but when the Gurkhas returned with the British they tore it down.

Fortunately, perhaps, we humans have short memories. Today, the great and brilliant Subhas Chandra Bose is only an incident in the minds of a small band of men and women who still consider him to have been one of India's noblest sons.

12
DEATH RAILWAY

More than 60,000 workers in January 1943 began to build a 428-kilometre-long railway linking Kanchanaburi in Thailand and Moulmein in Southern Burma. Half these workers were prisoners of war. It was a tremendously difficult operation which took nine months to complete. The cost in human lives was cruel.

It was reported at the war crimes trials held at the Victoria Memorial Hall in Singapore after the war that 3,600 Australian and 3,400 British prisoners died on that job. Casualties among the Asian civilian labour force are believed to have exceeded 10,000. It is thought that about 1,500 Japanese workers also never returned to their homeland. Indeed, this was the notorious Death Railway.

The railway was to transport supplies to Japanese forces in Burma; the Allies with their submarines had made it difficult for supplies to be sent by sea. Hence the order from the Supreme Command of Southern Army headquarters to link the Thai and Burma railway systems. No. 4 and No. 5 Special Japanese Railway Units were instructed to survey the area. Five thousand men of the Japanese National Railways were conscripted. They were not soldiers in name but were subject to rigid military discipline. Among them were civil engineers, railway engineers and technicians. They were organized into two groups. One group was sent to Thailand and the other to Burma.

The plan was to drive the railway though thick jungle. Most of the surveying was done from air. Bridges had to be built over streams and the River Kwai.

To find material for the railway, whole stretches of the line between Malacca and Tampin were pulled up and set to the construction sites. The track between Kota Bahru and Kuala Lipis was also taken.

Locomotives were dispatched from Japan and the Malayan Railway to operate on the new railroad. More than 300 goods wagons were operating on this line at its height. Railway tracks were brought down from Japan, Manchukuo (Manchuria) and Sumatra but the biggest stretch came from Malaya.

The problem was that many of the tracks were for different gauges but this did not bother the engineers. Their solution was simple indeed. They strung all the tracks on a metre gauge system regardless of whether the tracks were for large, medium or small gauge.

Feeding this large work force in the middle of nowhere presented tremendous problems, because in addition to the prisoners of war, there were civilian labour groups from Indonesia, Burma, Malaya and Singapore. The recruitment of labour from Singapore was short-lived. Of the few who worked there, many escaped and returned to Syonan.

Mutton and fish were practically impossible to get in quantity, so it was decided to drive a herd of 100 cattle from Burma right up to the construction camps. By now it had become obvious that the May deadline was unrealistic so the deadline was moved forward to August 1943, but even this was impossible to meet.

Because of the nature of the land, the cattle starved for most of the route, so much so that by the time they reached the camps there were only a few bags of bones contained in very filthy coverings of skin. Some of these emaciated carcasses were given to the Japanese soldiers in the area. They were delighted to receive this additional ration of very lean meat. Japanese soldiers and sentries always claimed that as bad as the prisoner of war food was, it was superior to what they ate.

Most of the cruelty and torture charges referred to at successive war crimes trials in Singapore after the war were based on the lack of food and the physical punishment meted out to the prisoners of war for alleged shirking, alleged insubordination and alleged attempts to escape from the working camps. There was also a criminal shortage of medicine, medical supplies and doctors.

It was adduced in evidence at the war crimes trials that Japanese sentries slapped, kicked, punched and behaved atrociously towards the prisoners of war who were on many occasions confined in bamboo cages like animals. But because of the different languages spoken, there was much misunderstanding. Finally the operation was completed; the railway tracks were linked and spiked on their sleepers. It was a supreme moment for everyone present, the Japanese, the prisoners of war and the Asian labourers. Here was the successful termination of a tremendous task. It was a thrill of success that nothing could stem. And over it all was a deep feeling of pathos for the thousands who had died while working on it.

The construction of this railroad was, in terms of lives lost, one of the most wasteful efforts in the Pacific War. Over and above the tremendous loss of Asian, Australian, British and Japanese lives must be added the lives of the following: Lieutenant-General Ishida, commander of the Thai end of the operation, Colonel Nakamura, Colonel Yanagida, Lieutenant-Colonel Ishii, Major Senda, Lieutenant-Colonel Banmo, Major Kudo and Lance-Corporal Onoda who were all sentenced to death by hanging.

The biggest price paid by Japan for the construction of this ill-reputed Death Railway is the enmity she earned from the local population, the British and the Australians. What is so shockingly ironical is that this railway, complete at such enormous cost in human lives and suffering, was operational for a relatively brief period.

It was completed at the time of the battle for Imphal— too late to influence the result of this battle. At the same time it became the target of successive bombings raids by the British and Americans. The link was bombed, repaired, bombed and repaired endlessly until it became useless when the British bombed the Burma railway out of existence.

The most useful purpose it served was to transport the retreating Japanese forces out of Burma at the end of the

Pacific War. Mr Subhas Chandra Bose also travelled along this line on his return to Syonan after his glimpse of India from the Burma border.

After the war the British decided to build a bridge over the Rappli River between Penang and Bangkok. They left the surveying for this bridge entirely in the hands of the Japanese prisoners of war special unit. The Rappli bridge was constructed with remarkable skill and speed. This is no surprise to any Japanese today, considering that the Japanese have constructed and are running the fastest rail service in the world between Tokyo, Osaka and Okayama.

13
ALLIED WAR HEROES

At five o' clock in the morning of 27 September 1943 terrific explosions were heard in the harbour. Minutes later, seven Japanese ships sank.

Then the sirens wailed, warning of an enemy attack. Japanese fighter-bombers took off and searched the Straits of Malacca and the seas to the south of Singapore, but no enemy vessels were sighted.

There were twenty large ships in the harbour at the time of the explosions. The thirteen still afloat moved out in a hurry.

The Kempei Tai declared an emergency and searched the city and the waterfront but found nothing to explain the explosions. Later they came to the conclusion that the ships had been sunk by mines fitted with timing devices attached to the ships by enemy frogmen. Much later they found out that this expedition had been led by Major Lyon of the Highland Infantry Battalion. He had escaped to Australia just before the fall of Singapore. With a party, he returned to Singapore in a dilapidated old vessel to blow up some ships in the harbour.

The Kempei Tai believed that the expedition must have been helped in some way, perhaps by secret correspondence with people in Singapore. Many Eurasians and Chinese, in consequence, were arrested on suspicion. The Sime Road Internment Camp was searched for shortwave radio sets. Some were discovered, and men were arrested and tortured; ten died. After the war, this episode was named the Double Tenth Massacre. Asians and Europeans were killed. It ranks with the massacre of the Chinese and the infamous Death Railway as one of the blackest pages in the story of the Japanese occupation in Singapore.

The success of Major Lyon's expedition caused the military authorities to set up several counter-espionage organizations immediately. There were, for example, the Army's *Nami Kikan* and the Navy's *Ushio Kikan*. Both groups controlled a number of junks and small boats. They were equipped with radios and sent out to patrol the waters around Singapore. *Nami Kikan* junks transported rice from Bangkok and Saigon. But they, too, became patrol boats. *Ushio Kikan* (Naval Intelligence) was commanded by Captain Hidaka. His headquarters was in Penang. *Nami Kikan* was commanded by Captain Yoshinaga. Besides the *Nami* and *Ushio* there was another counter-espionage unit known as *Ibaragi Kikan*. This was commanded by Major Ishijima.

The Army and police also set up observation posts along the coast. They were ordered to report to the Marine Kempei Tai immediately if they discovered any white men in the area. These observation posts extended all along the coasts of Sumatra, the Andaman and Nicobar Islands, the Riau Archipelago, and Linga and Singkep Islands to the south of Singapore. The Andaman and Nicobar Islands were commanded by Vice-Admiral T. Hara.

During this phase of the war Allied attacks became very effective in the Western Pacific. Japan lost Saipan and the Tojo cabinet resigned.

Allied submarines were sinking Japanese transports in an increasing number. In Syonan, people began moving out of the city.

On 10 October 1944, a year after the terrible Double Tenth bloodbath, the police in Kasoe Island, twelve miles south of Singapore, spotted a junk flying a Japanese flag. The crew were Australians. This report was immediately flashed to the Marine Kempei Tai. At once the Japanese launched a massive air and sea search for them. The searchers did not know it then, but Major Lyon had returned to try to blow up more Japanese ships in Singapore harbour.

He and his group came part of the way by submarine. In small boats this 'canoe flotilla' impudently sailed to Merapas Island in the Riau Group where food and supplies had been stored for them. They were to use this island as a base for raids on Singapore. Unfortunately for them, the police had already reported the discovery of the food and supplied, and a trap had been set for them by the Japanese.

I was told all about this after the Japanese surrender when, with Major Ishijima and Captain Yoshinaga, I was under detention by the British Field Security Force. Major Lyon died in a blaze of glory fighting a rear-guard action against heavy odds to allow his colleagues to escape. A Japanese officer and several soldiers were killed in this action. A group, most of them Australians, escaped and began island hopping in the Riau Archipelago.

They were pursued by Japanese troops for 120 miles. After losing a considerable number of officers and men, ten officer and soldiers of the sabotage party were captured on Singkep Island. They had run out of ammunition and food.

Because of their bravery, the ten survivors were treated as heroes by the Marine Kempei Tai. The Kempei Tai had remembered how well the Australian Navy and Government had treated the Japanese officers who had died in a raid on Sydney Harbour. They had been given a funeral with full military honours.

The ten Australian and British survivors were sent to Outram Prison and later faced charges of perfidy and espionage. They were kept in separate cells away from other prisoners. They were supplied with books, sweets and special foods. They were treated like heroes, for that, in the eyes of the Japanese military, was what they were.

I was told that had they petitioned the Japanese Army's Southern Command, as had been suggested to them, their lives would have been spared. They refused!

These men won the admiration of the all the Japanese officers and men connected with the case. A record of the trial held under Japanese military law showed that the chief judge was Major-General Ohtsuka. The prosecutor was Major Kamiya.

On the perfidy charge it was stated that they did not wear the proper uniforms of officers and men of the Allied forces. Evidence was given that some of them wore Malay clothing. Their faces and arms were dyed. Their junk flew a Japanese flag.

On the espionage charge it was alleged that they had collected information and had made photographs and sketches of enemy territory, etc.

Major Kamiya's closing address was emotional in a typically Japanese manner. 'With great determination,' he declared, 'they entered the area controlled by Japan. I have no hesitation in referring to them as heroes. Fortunately for us their plans were frustrated. Can you picture their unflinching devotion to duty, their bravery, without shedding a tear for them? The valorous spirit of these men reminds us of the attack on Sydney Harbour by our Special Naval Attack Unit, all of whom died early in May 1942. The Australian Government bestowed on those Japanese naval officers full military honours. We must return this honour to these heroes here. Their tremendous fighting spirit must be respected even though their mission failed. The last moment of a hero must be historic. It must be dramatic. And we must respect them, for heroes have a greater regard for their reputation than for anything else. So we feel it is our duty to glorify their last moments. We hope the names of these heroes will remain the hearts of the British and Australian people forever. In such circumstance I consider that a death sentence should be given to each of them.' It was 5 July 1945.

Major Ingleton, the senior officer among the survivors, stood up and thanked the Court for referring to them as patriots and heroes. He spoke on behalf of himself and the other nine prisoners. They were Captain E.C. Page, Lieutenant W.G. Carey, Warrant Officer A. Warren, Sergeant D.P. Gooley, Corporal C.M. Stewart, Corporal R.B. Fletcher, Lance-Corporal J.F. Hardy, Seaman W.C. Falls and Seaman F.W. Marsh.

Not everyone understood the prosecutor's closing address. Some non-Japanese thought it cruel, sadistic and barbarous. But to the Japanese, and those who understood the Japanese character, his remarks, and the sentence of death were the supreme accolade to which a hero could aspire. To a Japanese, to die in action or in the execution of his duty, is the highest honour one can achieve.

Two days after they were sentenced, the ten men were executed at Clementi Road. They all died bravely. They bade goodbye to each other. Some smiled at the Japanese They were buried under ten rough white wooden crosses After the war, their remains were removed to Kranji Military Cemetery.

After the execution, Major-General Ohtsuka issued a statement to the troops of the 7th Area Army. These men, he said, should be taken as models by all Japanese soldiers. He referred to their patriotism, fearless devotion to duty, their heroism 'and their sublime end ... like cherry blossoms falling off a tree'. Japanese soldiers should be inspired by the fine example set by these ten men. 'On reflection, they must feel the need to brace up their own spirits in emulation, if they hope to win the war.'

One special reason why Major Lyon's men were treated with so much respect by the Japanese was perhaps because so many Japanese remembered the terrific battle at Jamaluang near Mersing at the east coast of Malaya during the Japanese invasion of Malaya.

It was fought between 200 members of an Australian demolition party and a strong element of a Japanese brigade. The Australians were returning to Singapore after destroying Mersing Bridge and other bridges. Soon after dawn the Australians entered the mining town of Jamaluang and were surprised to see a large number of half-naked men moving about this small two-street place. They did not realize at first that these men were Japanese soldiers. They were part of the invasion force which had landed at Endau the week before. They were under the command of Colonel Kiba.

Almost simultaneously, the Japanese realized that the fully-armed Australians were ready for immediate action, and the demolition party recognized that the half-naked villagers were in fact the enemy. It was a fight to the death in which Saeki Tank Regiment from Kluang also took part. All 200 Australians were wiped out. The Japanese were reported to have lost a thousand men, killed and wounded.

The bravery of the Australians impressed the Japanese, especially their commanders, Colonel Kiba and Colonel Saeki. As a mark of respect they ordered a huge wooden cross to be set up over the mass grave of the 200 men on the side of a hill facing the north-east just outside Jamaluang, as the road curves to Mersing. On the cross were painted the words: 'To our Gallant Enemies, the Australians'. I saw this memorial on my first trip to Endau early in 1943. I have no doubt that many Japanese remembered the gallantry of this out-numbered band of Australians when Major Lyon's group of saboteurs was captured. Here, they must have said, was another band of brave men.

But Major-General Ohtsuka's exhortation to his men to be equally brave and devoted to duty 'if they hope to win the war' was too late. The war was nearing its end. Soon Syonan was being bombed in earnest by the Allies.

After the war, Lieutenant-Colonal Sumida, chief of the Syonan Kempei Tai, and many of his men were hanged in Changi Prison for the shameful parts they played in the Double Tenth Massacre. Win or lose, it's so vain!

14

EVACUATION OF
SYONAN ENDAU

In August 1943, Mayor Odate returned to Japan to become
Governor of Tokyo. At the same time the new mayor of
Singapore, Mr Naito, arrived in Syonan. Deputy Mayor
Toyoda was transferred to Shanghai where he became the
consul-general.

The emphasis now at military administration was
on self-sufficiency. Because of Allied activities, food was
becoming more scarce. The Grow More Food policy became
urgent. Syonan's population now stood at 1,000,000. It soon
became apparent that there was not enough land in Syonan
to grow the food to feed them. Consequently, the 7th Area
Army headquarters ordered that at least 300,000 people be
evacuated from Syonan.

This order from the 7th Area Army headquarters held
the rank of a battle operation order 'C-No. 1'. It was the
strongest order issued to Tokubetsu Shi during the war. It
read thus:

'The Syonan Tokubetsu Shi must execute this evacuation order immediately. The Military Administration Headquarters will assist the Tokubetsu Shi where necessary to implement it. The evacuation target is 300,000. Tokubetsu Shi shall select a suitable site to receive the people from Syonan. The necessary materials and transport will be provided by the Army.'

I knew that an evacuation scheme had been started in Tokyo. First the children left the city, then adults. But in Tokyo most of the evacuated went to stay with their relatives. Very few people in Singapore had relatives up-country. They would have to grow their own food: few of them had any farming experience. The new mayor placed the burden of the evacuation squarely on my shoulders. 'You organize it,' he said.

While I was in Changi Prison I had read the story of how Marshal Balboa of Italy had forced Italians to emigrate to the Libyan desert before World War Two. First he built houses, roads, wells and a water system. All this took him two years. Then, in 10,000-ton liners, he transported 10,000 settlers from Naples to Libya. This took him another year. My job was to force thousands of Syonans to emigrate to Malaya immediately.

How should I go about persuading them to leave? By telling them that Malaya would be safer that Syonan? By hinting that they would be moving away from Japanese military oppression? As long as they remained in Syonan they would always be near the dreaded Kempei Tai. Which line should I take?

I made up my mind, then went to see Lieutenant-Colonel

Mori, the staff officer at Army headquarters. I told him that force was out of the question. People had to be persuaded. My proposal was that we should work with the Overseas Chinese Association in building a Chinese settlement in which no Japanese would be permitted to set foot. There would be no Japanese guards or policemen. The Chinese themselves would make their own arrangements for law and order. Mori promised to submit the plan to higher authorities.

Satisfied, I then called a general meeting of the Overseas Chinese Association. I emphasized the following points: no Japanese would be allowed in the settlement; no Japanese law or regulation would apply—the settlement would be entirely self-governing; the Kempei Tai and the police would have no jurisdiction in the settlement; until the settlement became self-supporting the Tokubetsu Shi would supply rice. In case of trouble the settlement could always call upon my Welfare Department for assistance.

The association approved the idea and a New Syonan Model Farm Construction Committee was set up under the chairmanship of Dr Lim Boon Keng. Mr Chen Kee Sun was appointed general manager.

We had to find a good site, and so an Investigation Team was selected. This consisted of Chen Kee Sun, Tan Hoon Siang, Tan Eng Teck and Wu Mon Chew. The two Tans were agricultural experts. Lieutenant-Colonel Tajima from the military administration headquarters came with us. Our guard and driver was Sergeant Toyota. He was a notorious Kempei Tai soldier, later to be hanged. We set off for Malaya.

For ten days we searched for a site in Malacca, Negri Sembilan, Pahang and Johore. Finally we selected Endau in north-east Johore. The Overseas Chinese Association provided a million dollars for the construction fund. Work began at once. The military authorities were amazed at the speedy reaction of the Chinese community. Without delay the Construction Committee collected what seemed to be the finest jungle workers in Malaya. They worked with a will. We penetrated deep into the jungle. I slept with the workmen in their shanties in the jungle. The waters of the Endau River formed the north and north-eastern boundaries of the settlement.

When the big trees had been cut we waited a few days for the timber to dry, then we set fire to them. There were clouds of smoke everywhere; the smouldering *belukar* chased out the wild pigs and monkeys. After we had built a road, Dr Lim Boon Keng came to have a look at the progress we had made. He was impressed. We built an office at the entrance to the farm. Nearby was a small experimental farm where we cultivated Formosan rice and table vegetables, grown under the direction of Mr Tan Hoon Siang and his assistant.

Each settler was given a title to three acres of padi land and a vegetable patch. From the nurseries of the experimental farm he was given young plants. Padi land was given only to those prepared to cultivate padi. Soon the houses of the settlers were ready. We made preparations for the arrival of the first batch of migrants from Syonan.

In September 1943, ten lorries filled with settlers joyfully left the city steps on their 136-mile journey to New Syonan. There were no tearful farewells. On the contrary, there were shouts of joy. Everyone was happy: they were going to a place where everybody would be free.

I traveled with them on the top of one of the lorries. We stopped for lunch at Kota Tinggi and reached Endau in the evening. Carved out of deep jungle, the settlement looked like a giant bowl. Gentle sea breezes blew over the rice fields belonging to the Malay farmers nearby, causing the stalks to sway in an undulating motion.

A meal had been prepared for the settlers; they were allocated their new homes. And so the settlement developed, each new group being welcomed by the previous group. The settlement literally grew day by day, and a management committee had to be formed. This consisted of Chen Kee Sun, manager; Dr Hu Tsai Kuen and Dr Chen Ah Po, medical and health department; Robert Tan Hoon Siang, agricultural department; Low Peng Swee, supply department; Tan Kim Chiang, construction department; Wu Mon Chew, public works department; Leong Yuen Ho, timber mill; public peace and order, Wong Tatt Seng, later Lo Po Yee and G.H. Kiat.

Soon the settlement had a tool shop, a paper factory, a sawmill and, the Chinese being Chinese, several restaurants. Thousands of Singaporeans heard what was happening at New Syonan and applied to settle there, away from the constant pressure of the dreaded Kempei Tai. To show their appreciation, the settlers presented the settlement's first crop of rice to the mayor of Syonan.

But not enough rice could be grown in the settlement to feed everyone, so I went to Thailand to arrange for supplies of rice to be sent to Endau by lighters.

It was not long before the settlement opened its first school. Mr Martin Chen was in charge.

Gradually the population of New Syonan increased. The time had come for the settlement to have its own bank; the Overseas Chinese Banking Corporation opened a branch. Mr Lee Choon Seng, chairman of the bank, visited the settlement from time to time.

Mr Lee and Mr Yap Pheng Geck were traveling with Mr Hirose, Japan's Deputy Finance Minister, to Endau on an official visit when the anti-Japanese guerillas attacked. Mr Hirose's car was far ahead of Mr Lee's car. I was talking to Mr Hirose in the New Syonan office when Mr Yap rushed in with the news that Mr Lee had been shot and was in Mersing Hospital. I went at once to the hospital. Mr Lee showed me his Buddhist Association medallion which had been struck by the bullet. The bullet had ricocheted off the medallion into the side of his face. Mr Lee soon recovered.

This was the first time the guerillas had attacked officials of New Syonan. After that, convoys to the settlement were escorted by Japanese guards from the Kota Tinggi garrison.

A few months later, Mr Tan Yeng Teck and Mr Tay Ji Ai were shot dead by guerillas on the Mersing Road while traveling without escort to the settlement. I went to the Kota Tinggi police station with Mr Chen Kee Sun to clean the bodies and bring them back in coffins to Singapore.

Mr Wong Tatt Seng, the man responsible in the settlement for peace and order, was murdered by guerillas inside the settlement. It was a dark night with no moon. The guerillas ransacked the rice store. Another group of seven attacked Mr Wong's home near by. Mr Wong was killed by the first blast from the guerillas' tommy-gun. The gun was then turned on the children. Mrs Wong bravely stood in front of them. She faced the guerillas and demanded to know what the children were guilty of that they should be shot. The guerillas shot an 18-year-old girl and left.

Another victim of the guerillas' terror was Mr Lo Po Yee, who took over Mr Wong's duties in the settlement. Mr Lo was shot on the Kluang Road. I went to his funeral at the Thomson Road cemetery, and as the family threw earth on his coffin I asked myself why the guerillas killed their own people. Why did they not kill me, a Japanese? What irony that the Chinese in Singapore, seeking refuge from Japanese oppression, should be terrorized by Chinese guerillas.

I realized that if the terrorists kept up their attacks on the settlement the settlers would leave it. Already some were asking to return to Singapore. I decided to try and contact the guerillas to see if I could buy them off.

There was a small empty cottage not far from the settlement. It was by the side of the road. Occasionally I found anti-Japanese posters pasted on the walls. I left messages on the wall. In this way I succeeded in contacting them. I entered into an agreement with them. I gave them rice. In return they agreed to leave New Syonan alone. I kept this arrangement secret. I shared it with nobody. I knew that if it leaked out that I was contact with the guerillas I would lose my head. But in this way the settlement was saved. More people joined us from Singapore.

We named the streets after officials: there was Kee Sun Street, Boon Keng Street, and others. Shops were opened selling sweet potatoes and other vegetables grown by the settlers. One of the delicacies of New Syonan was lizard meat soup. It was cherry pink in colour and tasted like chicken.

The independence of the town—essentially a Chinese town—was carefully guarded. Once Johore policemen took away a settler on some frivolous charge. I immediately went to Johore and took him back to the settlement.

The main streets were brightly lit with gas lights. By the end of the first year, New Syonan had a population of 12,000. We celebrated with a concert by the police band sent from Singapore. We had Chinese operas organized by Mr R. Shaw.

The anniversary celebrations made the day worth remembering. On the main street were Hokkien and Cantonese operas. In the Plaza the police band played tunes like *Merry Widow and Over the Waves*. I felt like one of the settlers. I was very happy. I was invited to many homes by friendly groups of settlers. Then they carried me back to the settlement office, where I slept that night, happy in the knowledge that New Syonan was a success.

As the number of settlers increased the demand for more food also increased. I decided to go to Bangkok to arrange for the shipment of more rice. I organized a transport team and chartered lighters from the Izuka Iron Mine Co. Ltd. in Endau. Mr Kiat's son wanted to join the team. At first I refused but his father begged me to let him go, so I agreed. In Bangkok I met young Kiat buying souvenirs for his parents. Alas, they never received them, for on the voyage back to Endau the rice convoy was attacked by an American submarine. Most of the ships were sunk, and young Kiat was among those drowned.

I felt sad, but Mr Kiat accepted the loss bravely. 'I have lost my only son,' he said, 'but he gave his life for New Syonan.'

After the Japanese surrender, Mr P.T. Wong of the *Kosei-Ka* went to Endau. He found the settlement full of guerillas.

Mr Chen Kee Sun was 88 when I began writing this book, but he has since died. I believe Robert Tan Hoon Siang, Leong Yuen Ho, Dr Hu Tsai Kuen, Dr Chen Ah Po, Tan Kim Chiang, and other founders of the settlement are still alive.

Today, Endau is a Malaysian water-melon growing centre.

Right: Section of the Burma-Thailand railway showing cutting hewn out of solid rock, which rises hundreds of feet above Kwandi River, by prisoners of war. (Australian War Memorial)

Below: The interior of a typical 100-metre attap-roofed hut in a construction camp of the Burma-Thailand railway. (Australian War Memorial)

Above: An impressive silhouette of heavy cruisers on Singapore's seafront in April 1942.

Below: Major Lyon of the Highland Infantry Battalion (centre) who led a successful sabotage of Japanese ships in Singapore harbour. (Australian War Memorial)

Above: Syonan's soccer and hockey teams after a goodwill tour of Penang, Ipoh, Kuala Lumpur and Seremban, sponsored by the *Kosei-Ka*.

Below: People's consultation at the *Kosei-Ka*. Author is at centre.

Right: Bishop Devals, organizer of the Bahau settlement.

Below: The Endau Construction Committee with the author (second from left) about 30 years after the occupation.

Above: Mrs Lim Boon Keng, 1942.

Below: The author with Mrs Lim Boon Keng, 1972.

Last day at the *Kosei-Ka* (Welfare Department). The author is third from the left in the first row.

15

EVACUATION OF SYONAN BAHAU

We created a settlement for Eurasians and Catholics at Bahau in Negri Sembilan. Both the director of Industry and the head of the State Agricultural Department in Negri Sembilan had gained experience in Tokyo at the Ministry of Agriculture. They fully supported the Grow More Food campaign. They had opened several farms in the state. They invited the military administration in Singapore to send evacuees to the new farm they had recently created at Bahau. But the soil there was mostly clay, and there was not enough water to sustain a large population. Going to Negri Sembilan would also mean that once a Syonan went to Bahau he would cease to be a citizen of Singapore (which is what everyone in Singapore was during the Japanese occupation), and the City Government of Singapore would officially be unable to help them. Negri Sembilan would have to supply the tools, the seeds and the rice.

There was another great difference between Endau and Bahau. Endau was a self-governing settlement. The State

Government in Negri Sembilan decided not to permit this in Bahau. However, at the insistence of military headquarters which approved the scheme, wanting to get rid of as many people as they could from Singapore, community leaders and the Roman Catholic Bishop Devals agreed to send an Inspection Team to Bahau. The team consisted of Bishop Devals and Mr de Souza, Senior. They found the area cleared and several large huts already erected.

Frankly, I had qualms about the success of Bahau; enthusiasm for it seemed to be lacking. But the Catholics were renowned for their faith and I hoped that, with the leadership of Bishop Devals, all would end well. But the idealistic spirit that made Endau possible was missing from the start.

Bishop Devals decided to divide the settlers into two groups—the Eurasians (including a number of non-Catholics) and the Chinese Catholics. As a whole the settlers were educated; many of them belonged to the intelligentsia. But they did not have the money which the Overseas Chinese Association had. They moved by train from Singapore to the town of Bahau, and from Bahau to the settlement by lorry or on foot. I went with the first batch. They looked happy enough. Most of them were anxious to start building their own homes.

As soon as the huts were up they moved in, but there was no eagerness to start work on the land, and the Negri Sembilan Government complained to me about this. The basic difference between the policies which created the two settlements was that the aim of Singapore was to evacuate the people, whereas the main aim of the Negri Sembilan Government was to have more food grown.

My aim for Endau had been to make it a happy place for the settlers. I wanted the same for the Bahau settlers. The Negri Sembilan emphasis, however, was on the growing of more food. I repeatedly told them that the people from Singapore had no farming experience. I explained how, in New Syonan, we supplied the settlers with rice seedlings and young vegetable plants. The Negri Sembilan authorities made many promises but failed to carry them out. Instead, they complained constantly that the Singapore settlers were lazy.

Whatever else went wrong at Bahau, they had peace. There was no guerilla activity. Church bells pealed every morning and evening. Several convents moved out to Bahau. The sight of so many Fathers, Sisters and Brothers of the various Catholic Orders gave the impression of a settlement of Catholic priests and nuns.

There were several reasons why Bahau did not achieve the success of New Syonan. The soil was poor; there was not enough water. Malaria took the lives of many old people and children: the anti-malaria steps taken by the state authorities were inadequate. The Eurasians suffered most. Then the church bells tolled not to bring the faithful to worship but for the burial of yet another victim of malaria. I stayed in a small cottage for a few days and seemed to spend most of my time consoling bereaved families and handing out medicine.

I finally came to the conclusion that neither the Bishop's prayers nor my practical encouragement would help improve the situation. I decided, therefore, to top sending settlers to Bahau for the time being, until conditions got better. Newspapers reported the failure of the Bahau scheme.

I transferred the seriously sick back to Syonan. For a while my home in Singapore became a temporary hostel for those returning from Bahau.

In the settlement we did our best to organize anti-malaria teams among the younger settlers. They made some progress and some perhaps over-enthusiastic youngsters sought the permission of the Bishop to celebrate with a dance. The Bishop firmly rejected the idea. The youngsters were disappointed—they had had no fun since the settlement was opened. One of them openly rebelled and the Bishop promptly called in the police—which made the youngsters even more disappointed.

Hearing this, I hurried to Bahau and saw the Bishop. In the end he agreed to close an eye and permission was given for the dance to be held the following evening.

To enliven the proceedings I sent many bottles of Nanboku whisky, some rice, a bag of sugar and some tidbits. Meanwhile, the young men scrubbed and polished the dance floor. Every woman looked lovely. Where they had hidden the gay clothing they wore that night will never be known. The young men were clean and tidy. Everyone looked happy. The Bahau dance band played lively music and everybody danced. The old folk drank a glass of whisky, watched the youngsters, and for a brief while forgot malaria and their woes. Many of the sick rose from their beds and joined the party which went on until midnight.

In the hut next to the hall I could see the Bishop and some of the Fathers praying. The Bishop looked unhappy and I felt a deep sense of guilt. I saluted the holy man's shadow and returned to my small cottage. I rested on my bed. I could still hear the jazz music. As I got under my mosquito-net I felt rather sad and lonely. The Japanese authorities, I thought, would think that the settlers were concentrating on pleasure instead of planting padi. But, somehow, I thought that an evening's pleasant and harmless enjoyment and relaxation would brighten the lives of the young, perhaps put them in a better mood for work.

Gradually, there were fewer cases of malaria, and this, I am convinced, was because of the efforts of the anti-malaria teams. And so, once again, we sent more settlers from Singapore to Bahau. At the Great World Stadium the Syonan Sports Association organized a boxing match and gave the entire proceeds to the Bahau settlement.

On 17 January 1945 I received a report from Bahau that Bishop Devals had died suddenly. While cultivating his vegetable patch he had cut his foot with a hoe. Tetanus had set in and within days he was dead.

I sped to Bahau with Father Olcomendy (later to become Archbishop of Singapore and Malacca), but by the time we reached there the Bishop was in his coffin, resting in the church at Seremban. Bishop Devals at the time of his death was the highest-ranking Catholic prelate in the Malay Peninsula. He was a noble and fearless man.

He came to see me after the British surrender and later sought my help to rescue convent girls and Catholics in the Katong area and other places. As a consequence, we shifted all convents into the city area. I know that during the Japanese occupation he helped many people. He taught us how to love our enemies. Bishop Devals could have stayed in Singapore. He went to Bahau because he felt it was his duty to do so.

After the war I was told that he had advised Bahau's older settlers to stay quietly at Bahau until the Allied Forces came. 'Meanwhile,' he told them, 'Shinozaki and I will protect you.'

In spite of the fact that the war was still on, the Bishop's funeral was a very solemn affair. Many Roman Catholic priests from all parts of Malaya attended the service. I kissed the corner of the coffin because I had always held him in respect as a God-fearing man. Father Mussolini took over at Bahau.

Bahau made progress, although the Negri Sembilan Government got rather annoyed at all the help and attention we gave the settlement from Syonan. Night after night the train left Singapore with more settlers.

When the Japanese surrendered and I was detained in Balmoral Road, at the headquarters of British Field Security, Father Olcomendy, Father Mussolini, and other Catholic priests came to see me. They kindly submitted a petition to the British on my behalf.

When I came to Singapore in 1972 I called on Archbishop Olcomendy and Father Mussolini in Victoria Street. A few days later they came to see me at my place in Pasir Panjang Hill. We talked about old times. They were mixed memories.

16
ANOTHER SURRENDER

In 1945, the Americans bombed Malaya and Syonan. First they attacked Seletar Naval Base, then they bombed the city. The war was drawing to a close. Preparing for invasion, the Japanese formed the Japanese civilians into defence sections. For the first time, on the instructions of Army headquarters, Japanese women were given the rifle drill. The Japanese staff of the City Government were trained by an ex-Army officer, Mr Torii, of the Education Department. Nobody thought of surrender, not even I. We were all sure that the Japanese Army would fight the Allied forces if they tried to land.

The evacuation of civilians from Singapore was stepped up. Those remaining behind were organized into rescue and service groups under the direction of the Auxiliary Police.

I sent as much rice as I could to Endau, and I wondered if I should stay in Syonan or go to Endau or Bahau. Where did my duty lie?

The military script was losing value each passing day. Prices of food were going up hourly. But all was not gloom.

In the midst of this confusion a most lavish wedding party was held in the Adelphi Hotel to celebrate the marriage of the son of Choo Lye Huat (Kim Chwee) to Mr Lim Peng Mao's daughter.

Now, about the time, the Japanese warship *Takao*, damaged by a torpedo in the Mindoro Strait, had been towed to Seletar. Captain Onoda of the *Takao* came to see me. He said he had been appointed deputy chief of staff of the Southern Squadron. I told him about the wedding and invited him and his officers to attend. They arrived in their white dress uniforms, complete with golden insignia of rank and service ribbons. They added colour to an already colourful wedding. It was probably the last function attended by officers of the Japanese Imperial Navy wearing full dress.

On the west coast of Malaya, Allied liaison officers were being landed to contact the jungle guerrillas. Food, arms and ammunition were later brought in by parachute. The Kempei Tai intensified their activities. Major-General Lim Bo Seng and four of his officers were captured. Lim Bo Seng died in Batu Gajah jail. He was 35 years old.

News of the end of the war came suddenly from Tokyo. The Singapore garrison did not want to surrender. They had been trained to fight to the end, and this was what every soldier wanted to do. I am sure that if the Allied forces had invaded Singapore and Malaya the loss of lives on both sides would have been heavy. Thousands of civilians would probably have been Saipan, Iwojima and Attu all over again: there the Japanese had fought to the last man.

Had fighting broken out in Singapore the misery and loss of lives and damage to property would probably have been greater than in Manila. In Singapore, the Japanese were better armed and had enough rice to last them a year.

On the morning of 18 August 1945, General Itagaki, commander-in-chief of the 7th Area Army, ordered all commanding officers and civil officers (heads of departments) to his headquarters in Raffles College. He told them of the Emperor's decision to accept the Potsdam Declaration. He warned all officers and men to remain passive and not to start any recklessness. In the name of the Emperor he ordered them not to cause any trouble. 'Keep the peace,' he said.

Most of the Singapore garrison accepted the Emperor's decision. A few soldiers did not. They escaped with their arms and ammunition to neighbouring islands. They were caught and brought back to Singapore later.

Some people hoisted the Chinese national flag over their homes. Japanese soldiers angrily tore them down. I saw that a nasty situation could easily arise. So I decided to make a public announcement of the end of the war at the Majestic Theatre in New Bridge Road.

'There is no need now to evacuate to Bahau or Endau,' I told the audience. 'The war is over. The Emperor has accepted the Allied proposals. Peace has come at last. But, as you can see, there are many Japanese still armed and still willing to fight. This could lead to a dangerous situation. I therefore ask you to be peaceful and calm. Do not aggravate a dangerous situation. Do nothing rash. Wait patiently until the Allied forces arrive. Do not, meanwhile, put up flags.'

I left the theatre and was driven direct to the railway station to stop the evacuation train from leaving.

That night, pistol shots could be heard. Several officers decided to kill themselves rather than face surrender. Hand grenades were used for mass suicides.

The next day I was summoned to Army headquarters and severely reprimanded for announcing the end of the war without authority. Certain young officers threatened to kill me. I hid in the Poh Leong Kok (home of the rehabilitation of women) in Pearl's Hill. Two days later, Major-General Kamata, the General Officer Commanding Defence Headquarters, addressed his officers and men. He restored discipline.

I had just returned to my office when a young Chinese of about 35 years of age came in and said, to my utter astonishment, 'I am Chin from Chungking. I have been watching you for some time. Thank you for protecting our people. I am returning to Chungking. Would you like to come with me?'

I was amazed. Had he really been despatched from Chungking, lived in Singapore, and escaped arrest? I told him I appreciated his offer, but I would stay. There were still many things to do. I did not know what lay ahead. I might find myself back in Changi Prison once again, or this time I might be executed. No matter. I would prefer to stay.

He went away and I pondered. My conscience told me I had done nothing to be ashamed of. Some Japanese had accused me of helping the enemy. It was true I had taken the part of the people of Singapore against high-handed Japanese to such an extent that a gap had grown between my countrymen and myself. I felt that this was not my fault. I had carried out Mayor Odate's instructions to do what I could to look after the interests of the people. In doing this I believed I had done my duty to my country.

At Jurong, waiting for the British to arrive, the Japanese built themselves a concentration camp. We waited for two weeks. Meanwhile, municipal engineers built three cottages in the corner of the camp. The Japanese Army continued to maintain law and order, at least on the surface.

News of the surrender emboldened the guerrillas to come out of the jungle. They entered the towns and at first were welcomed as heroes. They sometimes attacked Japanese sentries, police stations and small garrisons, seeking to steal their arms. In parts of Johore, Negri Sembilan, and Perak, Japanese and guerrillas clashed, but the affairs were not serious. No punitive or retaliatory actions were taken. The Japanese moved out of the smaller towns into the larger towns. The guerrillas moved into the smaller towns in force and began dealing out summary justice to the police, the Kempei Tai, and the profiteers. There was terror and slaughter, and girls who had been mistresses of Japanese were among those who suffered. Many of those arrested by the guerrillas were marched or dragged through the streets and given a 'people's court' trial.

In Singapore, the guerrillas made the Japanese Club (now Selegie Complex) their headquarters. They began to prosecute collaborators, informers, and others whom they classified as traitors. Thus began a second period of terror and confusion for Singapore. Those able to do so fled to Hong Kong; some gave themselves up to the police, feeling safer in prison than outside.

Those were the days—no more than a few days, fortunately—of the Whispering Terror. Whispers could bring about death. Tan Boon Wu was stabbed in the heart because of a whisper. His body was left hanging on a tree. Wee Twee Kim, the Taiwanese, was another summarily executed.

The Japanese meanwhile had removed themselves to Jurong. The main elements of the Japanese Army moved to Kluang in Johore.

On 5 September 1945 the first units of the British Army landed on the seafront facing Collyer Quay. They were Gurkhas. I saw them land and watched them march to the Padang. They caught sight of the Indian National Army's memorial in the corner. They marched to it and levelled it to the ground. The crowd cheered. I felt a queer sensation in my stomach. I knew that this same crowd had cheered not long before when the memorial had been erected.

First, the Allied forces released the prisoners of war in Changi. Then they let out the inmates of the Sime Road Internment Camp.

Cases of cruelty reported by the prisoners and others resulted in some of the jailors and warders being arrested and taken to Outram Prison. The prisoners and the British civilians who had been in camps for more than three years at last came into the city. They were soon flown or shipped back to Britain.

Inevitably people sought revenge. Japanese policeman Wasai was well-known as a cruel man. He was a judo champion. He enjoyed tossing suspects about in the interrogation room. Often he tortured them with lighted cigarettes. He was arrested and taken to Outram Prison. There he was murdered. The Japanese superintendent of Outram Prison during the Japanese occupation found himself in one of his own cells. Tortured by ex-prisoners, he climbed up the iron-barred door. Someone outside took a photograph. It was published in a Singapore newspaper with the caption: Gorilla in Jail.

We handed over the city administration to the British military administration and were instructed to return the following morning. We assembled outside the mayor's residence. A young British officer inspected our belongings and tersely ordered, 'Go!' I led the march to Jurong. For seventeen miles we walked under the scorching sun, carrying the packs on our backs. The Japanese made the British walk to Changi. Now it was our turn. We walked without food. We arrived after dark, exhausted, but the camp staff were waiting, ready to receive us.

We civilian officials had been classified as Army personnel. We were not allowed to join the Japanese civilian community, not at first. Fortunately, we had among us water engineers, doctors, plumbers, electricians, and it was not long before we had electric light and water in the camp. Later we joined the civilians.

One day, after morning exercises, a jeep stopped at our camp. An officer and four soldiers stepped out. 'Is Shinozaki here?' called the officer.

I had been expecting the summons. I was ready for it. I stepped forward and identified myself. I was told to get into the jeep. I could feel the rounded tip of a tommy-gun in the small of my back. My Japanese friends stood in a line and said goodbye. When I passed the women and children there were tears in my eyes. I looked towards Changi and felt a sense of relief that the suspense was over. I expected to be executed.

17

JAPANESE REPATRIATION

I was taken to the Field Security Force in Balmoral Road, where I was kept in custody. I slept on a canvas bed. That evening a Chinese boy told me to accompany him to the dining room. Major Isaac, the Officer Commanding Field Security, smiled and pointed to the table where places had been laid for dinner. Most of the food came out of tins but it was tasty enough.

During the meal I asked the major when I should be returned to Changi. He told me there was no hurry. He said so many petitions on my behalf had been received, some from the highest sources, that my case was being considered. Meanwhile, I could stay at Field Security. I said I would like to do that and asked if I could have some clothes and books sent from Jurong. He said he would arrange for this. I requested that the mayor be informed that I was safe.

For the next few days I read books and lived a quiet life. Then Mr Blades, the man responsible for my arrest before the war, came to see me. Anticipating another period of interrogation, I felt uncomfortable, but he greeted me like a long-lost friend and said how grateful he was for the way I had been able to look after the people during the occupation. He asked me about Miss Yamakawa. She had been arrested in September 1940 but had not been charged. I told him that she had died in a ship sunk by an American submarine on the way back to Singapore.

Mr Blades said he had come to tell me that the authorities had decided not to put me back into prison to serve my unfinished sentence. I was grateful to him. I told him that I was bored with doing nothing. I offered my services as an interpreter. Thus, for the next two years, I was an interpreter in the British Army.

How strange our fates can be! The anti-Japanese forces had decreed that Shinozaki was not to be killed. Chin from Chungking had invited me to China. Now a British official, an ex-enemy, called to thank me for my work during the Japanese occupation. Some people understood what I had tried to do. Others disliked my activities, some even hated me, especially businessmen and those in the Japanese military. It is hard to be liked by both sides in a war. Major Hayashi had warned me, 'You are aiding the enemy.'

Had Japan won the war, I believe I might indeed have been charged with aiding the enemy, of being a traitor. I did not think of myself as such. I had done no more than try to be kind to the weak and helpless.

Now that Britain had won the war and I was working for the British Army, the Japanese were saying that I was a spineless fellow. This did not bother me. I was confident that with the passage of time the veils of hate would be lifted and the facts considered in the light of events and in their proper perspective.

The Field Security Force was mainly concerned with the activities of the Malayan communists. To get a full picture, Field Security took two Kempei Tai out of Changi. They were Sub-Lieutenant Yamaguchi and Sergeant-Major Shimomura. They were experts on the Malayan Communist Party. They were told to write all they knew about communist activities during the war.

After they had completed their reports, Colonel Davis, a liaison officer with the guerrillas, requested that they be returned to prison. At first Major Isaac refused, but pressure on him to do so increased when the remains of General Lim Bo Seng arrived in Singapore and preparations for the memorial service got under way. Reluctantly he returned them to Changi. These two Kempeis had been responsible for the arrest of General Lim Bo Seng.

General Lim Bo Seng's memorial service was held on 13 January 1946 in front of City Hall.

Altogether, Field Security interrogated some 400 Japanese. But much more than questioning was done by them. Indeed, in due course Field Security became the liaison centre for Japanese civilians. *Pro forma* passports for Japanese repatriates were issued. They were made in Jurong Camp and brought to Field Security for stamping. I usually took them back to the camp. There were many Japanese waiting to get back to Japan, both soldiers and civilians. The Japanese Army wanted to send back the troops first. I objected to this proposal and urged Major Isaac to send the civilians back first. He agreed.

There were 6,000 Japanese civilians in Jurong waiting to go home, but the 5,000-ton repatriation ship, the *Daian Maru*, had accommodation for only 3,444 persons. When the camp heard about this there was an uproar. Finally it was agreed to draw lots. All 3444 repatriates except thirty old ones walked the seventeen miles from Jurong to the harbour. They all made it; none fell by the wayside, so strong was the desire of all to return to their homeland. As for the thirty old ones, Major Isaac provided them with a lorry. They spent their last night in Singapore at Field Security headquarters with me. Major Isaac gave them biscuits and tea.

Though some in Singapore sought revenge, there were others with sympathy for the weak. In Jurong, few vegetables were available, and the women, especially those who were pregnant, suffered in consequence. I told Mr Mistri of the Phoenix Aerated Water Company about this. He promptly sent them a lorryload of vegetables, a gesture which was much appreciated by the camp.

Many Chinese visited the camp to look for their old employers and friends. Finally, the British arranged for a regular bus service for them.

After the first batch of Japanese had gone back to Japan, more Japanese from the camps up-country and from Java and Sumatra moved into Jurong, which became a transit camp.

There were human problems. Sergeant Rees came to me one day with several Chinese women. One held a baby in her arms. She said the baby's father was on a ship that had just left. The British, she said, had refused to allow her on board. She spoke in Japanese. Her husband was an employee of the

Syonan Sea Transport Company. They were legally married. Naturally she wanted to go with her husband.

She had made quite a scene at the wharf. I explained to her that she could go to Japan later, and that meanwhile she must wait at home.

'I have no home,' she said, 'I sold up, expecting to go to Japan. I cannot stay in Singapore. People are saying that I am a Japanese concubine.' Two other girls with similar problems also refused to go home. All three sobbed noisily.

After discussion with Major Isaac it was decided to send them to Jurong to stay in a corner of the camp. But when the news of this kindly act got out, about another thirty Chinese wives of Japanese demanded similar treatment. They lived together until we could finally ship them all quietly to Japan.

But there they ran into trouble almost right away, most of them, for they discovered to their dismay that their husbands were already married. This resulted in separation and a hunt for work. Some did very well for themselves. I know of one who found her husband unmarried to a Japanese. They worked together as hawkers. Today they own a big fruit market in the centre of Tokyo. They have five children.

I also know of a Chinese girl in Singapore who worked in a nightclub for five years to save enough money to fly to Tokyo to search for her Japanese husband. She took with her a basket of mangoes, her husband's favourite fruit. She came back after two weeks. She could not find him.

Lieutenant-General Numata, chief of staff of the Southern Army, and Captain Onoda, deputy chief of staff of the

Southern Army, stayed until the last Japanese left Singapore in order to maintain military discipline, something rather difficult to do at that time. Defeated troops are always more difficult to handle than victorious soldiers.

Some Japanese requested to stay. One was Mr Mori, a senior teacher at an English school in Kuala Lumpur. He had been a Selangor state soccer player. Field Security looked after all these problems.

At last my work was done. Repatriation was over, the war crimes trial completed. I returned to Japan. In appreciation of my work as an interpreter, the British military authorities gave me a pass enabling me to travel free on the Japanese railways. Japan was occupied by Allies and they controlled the railways.

18

DR PAGLAR'S
TREASON TRIAL

There are many injustices in a war, many misunderstandings, but some people's behaviour after the war I found to be inexplicable. Understandably, those who had co-operated with the Japanese during the occupation, often at personal sacrifice (some had no choice), became the targets for condemnation after the Japanese had surrendered.

Some of the community leaders, for example, found themselves vilified by the very people who had sheltered under their protective umbrella, made possible through co-operation with the Japanese.

I was ashamed at the treatment of my friend, Dr C.J. Paglar, president of the Eurasian Welfare Association. He was arrested by the British and charged with treason. He was jailed in Outram Prison. I was deeply touched to see his young wife carrying food for him to the prison every day.

On 26 January 1946, the trial of Dr Paglar began at the Civil District Court in Empress Place. The courtroom was crowded. Dr S.C. Goho, the first president of the Indian Independence League, and one of my ex-staff of the *Kosei-Ka* (Welfare Department), was present among the spectators. I was to be the prosecution's chief witness. My evidence would prove that Dr Paglar did co-operate with me, the enemy. I was in an awful position. I was determined to tell the truth, but I also knew that I must find some way to save my friend.

The newspapers at that time were also very much against Dr Paglar. This was the natural reaction. Every newspaper wrote very bad things against collaborators, calling them very big enemies of the people.

For the British this trial seemed to be of great importance. Some saw it as a means to recover the dignity of British officialdom which had committed the unpardonable sin of surrendering to the Japanese. They must recapture some of the dissipated dignity to prove that Great Britain was still a force to be reckoned with. Hence the importance of the trial.

Lieutenant-Colonel Peacock was the presiding judge. The prosecutor was Wing-Commander Cobbett. The defence was in the hands of Mr P.F. de Souza.

I was questioned by the prosecutor. I felt very nervous. I knew a lot depended on my answers.

He asked me what I knew about decapitated heads exhibited on spikes at several places in Singapore during the early days of the Japanese occupation.

I told him about the looting. I told him how eight Chinese had killed a Japanese sentry and entered a military store. They had been caught red-handed and were arrested by

Japanese soldiers. They were immediately executed. Their heads were exhibited with a notice about their crimes.

Mr de Souza: 'If anybody disobeyed the orders of the military would they receive similar punishment?'

I replied: 'During the early days of the occupation, they would.'

Mr de Souza: 'The people had to obey the orders of the military government?'

'Yes.'

Mr de Souza: 'The prosecution has stated that the message read by the accused on the behalf of the Japanese Emperor was treason against the United Kingdom because he is a British subject. What do you have to say about that?'

'The Army ordered the birthday celebrations. I relayed the order to the community leaders. Each community had a slightly different version of the birthday message which I wrote myself. The leaders had to read these messages to carry out my (military) orders.'

Mr de Souza: 'You are a good friend of the accused?'

'I am. And I am hurt to see him in such trouble.' I continued, 'We Japanese were like a stepfather after the real father, the British, left their children behind. The stepfather was brutal—the community leaders shared with them the responsibility of looking after these children. Now, alas, the real father has returned and is blaming these leaders for obeying their stepfather. Instead they should be praising them for their protection.'

I took a deep breath and told the judge, 'I was the one who directed Dr Paglar. He followed my guidance the whole time. I did this because I knew the grave position of the Eurasian community. I regret to see Dr Paglar in this trouble—the responsibility for what he did was mine. If anyone is to be punished, please punish me, not Dr Paglar.'

There was complete silence in the courtoom when I finished talking and broke down.

The prosecutor looked at me. He opened his mouth to speak, but said nothing. Mr de Souza stood up. He told the judge he had nothing to add.

British soldiers escorted me out. I had no regrets. I had thought of taking my life after the surrender. Perhaps now was a good time to die, to compensate in a small way for all the atrocities committed by my countrymen.

Dr Paglar was freed, the Court deciding not to proceed with the trial. It was an unusual verdict, the judge saying that the trial stood adjourned until the accused's natural death.

I was relieved. I felt that the British were still a great people. They had kept their dignity. Thinking people realized that in their traditionally bungling style they had emerged from this interlude with some respect still left.

There were no more trials of community leaders. All the charges were dropped. It was a wise decision. Dr Paglar passed away on 9 December 1954 following a heart attack.

19

WAR CRIMES TRIALS

Now came the war crimes trials. They took a few years as many Japanese war criminals were put on trial. About 135 were executed, all of them at Changi.

Lieutenant-General S. Fukuyei, commander of the prisoners of war camp in 1942, was the first to be tried. He had ordered two Australian and two British soldiers to be shot. They were shot on the shore at Changi. Fukuyei was sentenced to be shot at the same place. Singapore newspapers published a photograph of the execution.

Next, Vice-Admiral T. Hara, the General Officer Commanding the Andaman and Nicobar Islands, and five of his men were found guilty of murdering nine Burmese in July 1945. They were all hanged on 19 June 1946 with two Kempeis, Yamaguchi and Shimomura. I had known the two Kempeis for some time, and had worked with them on the Malayan Communist Party files in the Field Security Section.

On the eve of their execution Sergeant Rees and I went to see them, to check up a point in their reports. A Canadian soldier took us to the same lock-up where I had awaited my fate just before the fall of Singapore. The Chinese poem I had scratched on the wall had been scrubbed off. Iron grilling formed the other three sides of this cell.

The two condemned men gave me a poem they had composed about the impending doom—their last thoughts—and requested me to forward it to their families in Japan.

One of them said, 'Now we climb the thirteen last steps and shout "Long live the Emperor!"'

I offered them boiled eggs and tea, but they had no appetite. We said goodbye. A few steps away we passed Vice-Admiral Hara's cell. He looked up. I saluted him. He smiled. He looked calm, resigned to his death the following morning. He had accepted responsibility for the murder by his men of the nine Burmese because, he said, he was their commanding officer.

Many families and relatives of victims of the Death Railway came from Australia, some even from England, to attend the trial of officers and men accused of crimes in connection with that tragic page of history. They saw Lieutenant Ishida, the General Officer Commanding of the Thai end of the railway, sentenced to death together with many others including Colonel Nakamura, Colonel Yanagida, Lieutenant-Colonel Ishii and Major Senda. Many Japanese medical officers were sentenced to long terms in prison, some to life imprisonment. At the trial of prisoners of war camp personnel, Major-General Saito, Captain Suzuki and Tominaga, Kobayashi and Kawazoye were sentenced to death by hanging.

Some of the Chinese newspapers were reporting that soon the trials of those Japanese responsible for the massacre of Chinese civilians would begin. A few of these reports highly exaggerated what had happened (which was bad enough) and they aroused a great deal of Chinese hatred and anger.

These trials, involving a large number of Japanese officers, began on 10 March 1947. Colonel Sugita and I were summoned as witnesses. Colonel Sugita had been the Intelligence staff officer of the 25th Army under General Yamashita. He had been one of the officers who had escorted General Percival to the place along Bukit Timah Road where General Yamashita awaited the British surrender. Colonel Sugita was the only one of the 25th Army staff officers to be still alive. When he was brought to me at Field Security he was emaciated. Later, Lieutenant-General Nishimura, the former General Officer Commanding the Imperial Guards Division, came to Field Security. He was to stand trial and Colonel Sugita was to give evidence against him.

When I woke up one morning I saw that Colonel Sugita's bed was empty. There was a note on my table. I read it and rushed out of the room to search for him.

At the back of the house I heard a groan. There he was, sitting on the ground with his face towards the north-east. His neck was smothered in blood. He stretched back, still trying to cut the carotid (two arteries) with a blunt stainless steel table knife. His hand was trembling violently. I sprang on him and wrenched the knife away.

Sergeant Phillips was on duty. Together we carried the colonel to a jeep and sped to Alexandra Military Hospital. I held a blood-soaked towel to his neck. He was unconscious and his feeble breath whistled through his throat like a high-pitched note from a flute. He seemed to be in a serious condition, but three days later he was out of danger.

His note had read, 'I cannot bear to give evidence against my senior officer. I prefer to kill myself than be a witness for the prosecution. Best regards to our British friends.'

When Lieutenant-General Nishimura saw this note he said he understood. Sugita, he knew, would have found it difficult to give evidence against him.

In his tent, Lieutenant-General Nishimura wrote the whole day long about the activities of his division during the Malaysian campaign.

He was the most senior among the accused officers at the trial of those involved in the massacre of the Chinese. Others were Lieutenant-General S. Kawamura of Defence headquarters, and the Kempei Tai officers, Lieutenant-Colonel Oishi, Lieutenant-Colonel M. Yokota, Lieutenant-Colonel T. Jyo, Major S. Onishi, and Captain Hisamatsu. Captain Goshi, former Kempei Tai chief at River Valley, had already been sentenced to hang in Kuala Lumpur.

The floor of the courtroom was filled with Chinese. I recognized Mr Wu Pack Sin, the Chinese consul-general, among the spectators.

Lieutenant-Colonel Forsythe was the presiding judge. He had four assessors. Major Fulcher was the prosecutor, assisted by Major Ward. A Japanese lawyer, Mr Kurose, appeared for the defence.

The prosecution said that massacres had taken place at the seaside at Punggol, the seaside at the tenth mile on the

Changi Road, and the sea off Pulau Belakang Mati (now called Sentosa).

Lieutenant-Colonel Forsythe explained that the city area came under the command of the 5th Division of the Japanese Army, the west under the 18th Division, and the east under the Imperial Guards Division.

Colonel Sugita was the first witness. He was questioned by Major Ward about conditions at that time in Singapore. Colonel Sugita described the disturbances, the looting, the fires, the explosion of ammunition dumps. He said that the Chinese volunteers had disappeared immediately after the British surrender. They had all gone underground. To maintain peace and order, the Army headquarters had decided to clean up Singapore by picking up communists, volunteers and anti-Japanese elements.

Replying to another question, Colonel Sugita said the total number of Chinese victims in the city area was estimated to be about 5,000. There may have been another thousand victims in the eastern sector of Singapore.

I was the next witness. I was asked how many Chinese had been able to rescue from the various concentration camps, how many protection cards I had been able to issue for them. I could not tell Major Ward exactly—at least 2,000. Many more probably, counting the busloads of Catholics from Upper Serangoon and Katong.

Major Ward questioned me about these street concentration camps. Were there any shelters? None, I replied. The victims stood and sat in the sun, especially in the camp near River Valley Road. In the camps at Serangoon Road and Paya Lebar there was a littler shelter for a few under the branches of rubber trees.

Mr Kurose, counsel for the defence, cross-examined. He wanted to know about the protection cards. Under whose authority were they issued? I told him they were issued by me with the approval of the Defence Commander, Lieutenant-General Kawamura. I explained that I was the only official of the Japanese Foreign Ministry in Singapore at the time of Operation Clean-up. There was no other Japanese civilian in Singapore at the time. I told him that I had issued the protection cards to Germans, Italians, Thais, Swiss and other foreigners. When the Chinese heard about these cards they came to me for help. And that was how I came to be issuing cards freely to all asking for them. I stamped to the cards: SPECIAL FOREIGN AFFAIRS OFFICER OF DEFENCE HEADQUARTERS. I accepted full responsibility for the cards. I printed several thousands of them and signed each one I gave away. Each card stated that the bearer of the pass was a good citizen and requested Japanese soldiers to 'please look after him and protect him'. Despite its simplicity, perhaps because of it, this card was recognized and respected by the Japanese soldiers.

Mr Kurose: 'How many did you issue?'

I replied, 'Between 20,000 and 30,000 during the early days of the occupation.'

'To whom did you issue them?'

'To everyone asking for them. I gave hundreds to community leaders to distribute. I made no attempt to find out whether they went to communists or anti-Japanese elements or bad hats.'

Mr Kurose questioned me about the Overseas Chinese Association. I explained that it was formed to protect the Chinese community and that it assumed functions similar to those of the Chinese Chamber of Commerce.

On 14 March 1947, the sole survivor of the Tanah Merah massacre gave evidence. He was Mr Tan. He said the victims were told to wade out to sea. When the water was chest-high, Japanese machine-gunners opened fire. He was shot in the arm. He pretended to be dead. When it was dark he crawled ashore and hid.

Then another witness, a survivor of the massacre off Pulau Belakang Mati, gave evidence. He told the Court that several hundred Chinese were put into boats which were towed out to sea by a tug. Off the island they were thrown into the sea and machine-gunned. Patches of the sea quickly became stained with blood.

A Japanese witness brought from Japan gave details of the operation order. It had been made out by Major Hayashi, staff officer at Army headquarters. He had been temporarily attached to Defence headquarters for this operation. The order was passed to the Kempei Tai for execution.

No one could tell the Court who ordered the operation to be stopped. I am now able to reveal that Major-General Manaki, deputy chief of general staff, gave this order.

I am also now able to reveal that the operation had been planned by the Operation Staff of the 25th Army headquarters and ordered in the name of General Yamashita, the commander-in-chief, to be carried out by Defence headquarters. Defence headquarters delegated the Kempei Tai to carry out this foul job.

During the period of the Japanese occupation the number of victims in the Chinese massacre was a top secret affair. After the war Kempei Tai reports and other evidence revealed that the total was probably 6,000. In addition, another 9,000 died during the bombing of Singapore. The number executed at Outram Prison was 147 and 1,470 died in the prison from other causes. Altogether I believe the number of Chinese victims in Singapore during the Japanese occupation to be around 17,000.

On 2 April 1947 the trials ended. Lieutenant-General Kawamura and Lieutenant-Colonel Oishi were sentenced to be hanged. Lieutenant-General Nishimura was ordered to be imprisoned for life, but he was taken to Australia to face other charges. There he was accused of murdering 150 Australian and 35 Indian soldiers who had surrendered at Bakri near Batu Pahat in Johore. He was found guilty and hanged on 22 June 1950.

Others who received life sentences for the parts they played in the massacre of the Chinese in Singapore were Lieutenant-Colonel Yokota, Lieutenant-Colonel Jyo, Major S. Onishi and Captain Hisamatsu.

After the trials I was told that Lieutenant-General Kawamura agreed that the sentence of death passed on him was reasonable. He said that he was guilty. Yet, curiously, he was a kind-hearted man. But he was a soldier, and orders were orders. While he was in Changi Prison waiting for death he wrote a book, *Going Up the 13 Stairs*, at the east corner of Changi Prison. In the book he describes his trial, and also mentioned the Overseas Chinese Association and my connection with it.

After the war, superstitious people said that the atom bomb blasting of Hiroshima and Nagazaki was a punishment from Heaven. Operation Clean-up, they said, had been carried out by an infantry from the 5th Division of the Hiroshima area which had acted as supplementary Kempei Tai during the massacres. The 18th Division, noted for its ferocity during the massacres, came from the Nagasaki area.

Perhaps they were right: God does indeed move in mysterious ways.

Above: The Japanese marching to another surrender on 12 September 1945.

Below: Signing the surrender papers at City Hall, Singapore. Lord Mountbatten is second from the left in the row of British officers facing the camera. General Itagaki is fourth from the left in the row of Japanese officers.

Right: Dr C.J. Paglar.
Below: Judges at the war crimes trials.

Right: Japanese war criminals being escorted to the dock in Victoria Memorial Hall on 10 March 1947. (from left to right) soldier, Lieutenant-General Nishimura, soldier, Lieutenant-General Kawamura, Colonel Oishi.

Below Left: The author as witness.

Below Right: Colonel Sugita as witness.

Lieutenant-General Shinpei Fukuyei, commander of the prisoner of war camps in Singapore and Malaya during the occupation, was told to point out the place where British prisoners of war were executed. He was later shot at the same spot on Changi Beach in April 1946.

Banana money. The emphasis on growing more food during the occupation is depicted here.

A tombstone at the Japanese cemetry at Chuan Hoe Avenue for more than 10,000 Japanese soldiers and civilians who died between September 1945 and April 1947.

20

EPISODES

Memories keep coming back... The City Government was ordered to remove the statue of Raffles. 'Destroy it,' ordered the Army. Marquis Tokugawa, director of the museum, put the statue in his storeroom and reported that he had destroyed it. After the Japanese surrender he put it back on its pedestal.

Big-headed staff officers directed that 'Stamford Road' be changed the 'Yamashita Road'. The general himself vetoed this directive.

Other staff officers ordered the Kempei Tai to treat the Eurasians as semi-enemy personnel. They should carry out a census of this group. Eurasian families with British or Dutch fathers must be interned. Lieutenant-Colonel Yokota gathered about 7,000 Eurasians on the Padang. He told them to collect their census cards from the Toyo Hotel. I was staying at this hotel and I helped carry out this census-cum-registration. Sons and daughters of British or Dutch fathers were told to go to the internment camps at their convenience.

But this did not satisfy the Army. Mr K. Wada was appointed Controller of Enemy Persons and directly he issued these Eurasians with red armbands. This marked the wearer as enemy personnel.

This meant that these Eurasians were under the constant eye of the Kempei Tai, a most unpleasant experience. Finally, to their relief, they were all interned. When the British returned and they were released, some told me that they preferred being inside the camp than in the city under the menacing eye of the Kempei Tai.

The Japanese Army in mid-1942 conceived the idea of building a Shinto shrine. They put 20,000 Allied prisoners to work under the direction of the Yokoyama Engineering Regiment. The shrine was put up at the western end of MacRitchie Reservoir, near Sime Road. It was made to look like the Ise Grand Shrine in Japan. There were jungle trees and a beautiful red bridge across a small river, just like at Nikko.

Wearing the official uniform of a thousand years ago, in black to indicate his high rank, Mayor Odate performed the opening ceremony early in 1943. Other officials wore red and blue uniforms in accordance with their rank. They all wore wooden shoes. Generals, admirals, senior officials and businessmen were all in attendance. So were community leaders and priests of other faiths. They all followed the manner of the Japanese at prayer. I explained to them that the ceremony showed respect for the ancestors of the Japanese Emperor. 'You can learn something about Japanese customs from this ceremony,' I told them. 'You do not betray your religion.'

Many Japanese and Singapore people visited the shrine as they do the Ise Grand Shrine in Japan today, but just before the surrender, the Japanese Army destroyed it. I recall that it was just after finishing work on this rather beautiful construction that the Allied prisoners were sent to Thailand to work on the notorious Death Railway.

Colonel Koda was the commanding officer of the Selangor garrison. He used his position to make money. He bred pigs in the grounds of the barracks. He kept pestering the Chinese for gifts. He lived with a European woman called Doris. The Kempei Tai eventually arrested her as a spy. In January 1943 she jumped out of, or was thrown out of, the second floor window of the Kempei Tai headquarters in Kuala Lumpur. The Kempei Tai reported that she had committed suicide while being questioned about her spying activities.

Soon afterwards, Colonel Koda was arrested, court-martialled and sentenced to three years imprisonment. He was demoted to private and was summoned to Japan to serve his sentence. When the Japanese surrendered he was summoned to Malaya to be a witness in a war crimes trial. But he disappeared.

In subsequent investigations by the British it was established that Doris was an Italian with the Dutch-sounding name of Van der Straaten. She insisted that she was Australian. It seems, according to what a Kempei Tai interpreter said, that while being questioned by the Kempei Tai she was slapped by Sergeant Murakami. She promptly slapped him back. Losing his temper, Murakami had grabbed her and thrown her out of the window. The interpreter confessed that the story about her being a spy had been concocted in order that the Kempei Tai could prosecute Colonel Koda.

I was in Jurong Camp when General Itagaki, accompanied by his staff officers, all of them minus their swords and insignias, climbed the City Hall steps to attend the surrender ceremony. After the ceremony (on 12 September 1945) Lord Mountbatten told the press that he would have liked to have had Field-Marshal Terauchi, commander-in-chief of the Southern Army, sign the surrender documents, but this was not possible because Terauchi was ill. Lord Mountbatten remarked that this was regrettable because he would have liked to have taken the field-marshal's sword.

When Terauchi heard this he at once came to Singapore with his sword for Lord Mountbatten. He was still a very sick man and he died in Singapore shortly afterwards. His ashes were buried in Japanese tomb in Chuan Hoe Avenue, off Yio Chu Kang Road.

Having signed the surrender documents, General Itagaki was sent to Tokyo to stand trial with General Tojo, General Dohihara, General Matsui and others. General Itagaki was among those executed.

All Japanese civilians in Singapore and Malaya were concentrated in Jurong after Japan's surrender. There they waited for a ship to Japan. Among them were some who had lived in Singapore or Malaya most of their lives. Some had done well, had property and small fortunes. Now these had been taken over by the British Custodian of Enemy Property.

All the Japanese had to show for their years in Singapore and Malaya were bundlers of Japanese script, banana money it was called, and perhaps a savings book in yen. In Jurong Camp they were told to burn the banana money because it was now worthless.

Those Japanese who had lived in these parts all their lives could hardly bear to do this: this money represented their life savings. Some burnt the money and then hanged themselves from nearby rubber trees. They could not face a new life, penniless, in Japan. Others, made of sterner stuff, went back and some made good.

Forty people were buried in Jurong while the camp was in operation.

During the Japanese occupation the Home for the Aged managed by the Little Sisters of the Poor was looked after by the Welfare Department, so I was well-known there. After the surrender I was told that an old Japanese couple in the Home wished to see me. I was driven there in a jeep by a British N.C.O. The couple told me that they had been interned in India. When they came back to Singapore everything was gone. Since then they had been inmates of the Home. Now that Japan had been defeated they feared they would be sent to Japan. They had no relatives there. Could they be allowed to stay in the Home? The Father said he had no objections provided the British authorities did not object.

Field Security obtained permission for them to stay. Years later, I again visited the Home for the Aged in Thomson Road. I asked about them and was told they were sleeping peacefully in a Catholic graveyard behind the Home.

In August 1946, British headquarters wanted a series of lectures to be given to young officers about to go to Japan as part of the Allied occupation forces. Some of them were not long out of Oxford and Cambridge. I was to lecture on the history of Japan since the Meiji Restoration a hundred years ago. I was to deal with politics, economics, the military and general social conditions. The lectures were to last a week.

The difficulty was that I had no reference books except the book, *Whirlwind 20 Years*. This had been published by the newspaper *Mainichi Shimbun* immediately after the war. So I had to go to Changi Prison once again to borrow some of the thousand books I had sent to the Japanese prisoners. Those books had been part of my own library.

About eighty young officers were waiting for me in a lecture hall. They were commanded by a group captain. As I stepped on the dais, an officer shouted, 'Stand up! Attention!' I saluted and began my lecture.

In spite of the poor standard of English I lectured from nine in the morning until five in the afternoon every day. I had an eager audience. On the last day, I answered questions. Most of them were about Japanese customs.

When the course was over, a young officer shouted, 'Stand up! Attention!' Turning to me, the group captain expressed his thanks.

I could not help comparing my treatment as a prisoner of the British with the treatment given to prisoners of the Japanese. I felt ashamed that the Japanese had not behaved like this. Perhaps this was one of the reasons we were defeated.

Shortly afterwards, the group was sent to Japan to be stationed in the western part of the country. I thought I would never see them again, but I did meet one of my class in the Marunouchi Hotel in Tokyo. It was Captain Roberts. He recognized me. He said that my lectures had proved very useful.

Early in 1947 I went to Saigon to give evidence. I sailed from Singapore in a French transport ship. It was a pleasant voyage. In Saigon I was put in the officers' camp outside the city and shared a hut with Lieutenant-Colonel Kamiyoshi and Captain Konishi, the French-speaking liaison officer. Major-General Manaki, Syonan's first military administrator, was in Saigon Jail. As I wrote earlier in this book, I sent him some cigarettes and toilet paper in the name of the Overseas Chinese Association as a small token for his past attitude to the association and the Chinese community.

My work in Saigon took me just thirty minutes. I wrote a report and signed it. Forty days later I was back in Singapore having enjoyed what was almost a holiday.

French Indo-China was already rumbling: the Vietnam problems were already shaping up.

After the surrender, Japanese soldiers were put on the labour force. They worked at Keppel Harbour, Bukit Timah and Paya Lebar Airport. Paya Lebar Airport had been started by Allied prisoners of war who returned to Changi Prison from the Death Railway. After the surrender this construction was carried out by Japanese prisoners of war.

All of them, totalling about 30,000 to 40,000, stayed in various camps in Upper Changi Road, Seletar, Nee Soon, Keppel Harbour and the hillside of Clementi Road. I stayed for a month in the camp near Keppel Harbour. Soldiers worked in the wharf for loading and unloading. All of them were very hungry. Some attacked the military store and stole food. There were no vegetables in the Keppel Harbour camp and many came down with beri-beri. The other camps cultivated vegetables, but many of the inmates suffered from malaria. Sick persons were sent to the Nee Soon temporary military hospital where many died. Smoke from the cremations could be seen every day.

The prisoners of war remained in these camps until the end of 1947. Before their repatriation, they cleaned the Japanese cemetery in Chuan Hoe Avenue off Yio Chu Kang Road and set up Field-Marshal Terauchi's tombstone in the eastern corner of the cemetery, then they built three tombstones in the western corner of the cemetery with this inscription:

'In memory of the souls of the Labour Force comprising Army and Navy personnel who died in Singapore between September 1945 and April 1947.'

Behind this memorial, the ashes of more than 10,000 Japanese prisoners of war were put into a hole which was sealed with concrete.

There is a small concrete pillar which marks the spot where the ashes of the 135 Japanese officers and men who were executed at Changi Prison are buried. In the corner of the west end, there is another small concrete pillar which marks the burial spot of the ashes of 79 Japanese who were executed in Malaysia.